Let The Good Times Roll

An Anthology of Indiana Music

by

Larry Goshen

with

Mark Shaw

Foreword

by

Buddy Montgomery

Let The Good Times Roll, A Books For Life Foundation Publication, Copyright, 2002, Mark Shaw and Larry Goshen, 1060 Virginia Avenue, Indianapolis, Indiana 46203, 317-685-2500. Foundation Website: booksforlifefoundation.com.

Mark Shaw 1945-
Larry Goshen 1941-
     Let The Good Times Roll, An Anthology of Indiana Music by Larry Goshen and Mark Shaw
     p. cm.
  ISBN 0-9717596-2-6
     1. Shaw, Mark 1945- . 2. Goshen, Larry 1941-   . 3. Music 4. Music History
     5. Indiana 6. Indiana Music History I. Title

First Edition

10 9 8 7 6 5 4 3 2 1

International Standard Book Number – 0-9717596-2-6

Printed by Mentzer Printing Ink, Indianapolis, Indiana, USA

Cover Photograph of "Pookie" Johnson by Larry Goshen

Dedicated To:

Larry Goshen's Friends

"Bouncin' Bill" Baker,
The Inspiration For Many Young Musicians

and

Paul Gray

Acknowledgments

Larry Goshen thanks the many musicians and entertainers who provided their time and effort to contribute to Let The Good Times Roll.

They include good friend Don Kelley. His many years of friendship and encouragement (and work without pay) helped make this book a reality. With out his helpful push, "I know you can do it attitude!" and generous help, I could not have completed the book.

I extend special thanks to other encouraging friends and family. They include my daughter Renee, sons Mark and Larry, Cathy Morris, Yun Hui, Bill Baker, Mauvene Borton, Chris Conrad, Jan Fiscus, Jennie DeVoe, Leta Essig, Monica Herzig, Peter Kienle, Robin Holm, David Wright, Gary Walters, Mike McKenna, JoEllen Nuftul, Michael Coutts, Linton Calvert, Mary Sexson, Scott & Chona Stewart, Brian Morris, Jennifer Dixon, Melissa Bruhn, Chris Winkle and Dan Garver of Ritz Camera Center, Mentzer Printing, and the employees of Firehouse photograph service.

Mark Shaw thanks his wife Chris for her love, support and editing skills, and Amy Lain and Bis Whitacre for their assistance with the book. He also thanks Linton Calvert for introducing him to Larry Goshen, Indiana's finest musical historian, and John T. Lupton for his friendship and generosity as the founding benefactor of Books For Life Foundation, an organization dedicated to helping aspiring authors help themselves. Above all, Mark thanks the Good Lord for his true blessing in permitting him to collaborate on this book.

Mark Shaw Books

Let The Good Times Roll
Miscarriage of Justice, The Jonathon Pollard Story
Book Report, Helping Aspiring Authors Help Themselves
Melvin Belli, The Lawyer, The Legend, The Defender of Jack Ruby
Par For The Course
Larry Legend
Testament To Courage
Jack Nicklaus, Golf's Greatest Champion
The Perfect Yankee
Forever Flying
Bury Me In A Pot Bunker
Diamonds In The Rough
Down For The Count

Table Of Contents

Praise For Let The Good Times Roll

Let The Good Times Roll features over three hundred and fifty artists that contributed to Indiana's music scene. Covering five decades, music historian Larry Goshen's compilations of music history began seventeen years ago with the publication of *Indy's Heart of Rock 'n' Roll*. Utilizing his expertise as a photographer, music historian, and love of music as a performer, Larry has bettered that book with this one.

Combining his photographic talent with the writing efforts of author Mark Shaw, Goshen presents fascinating information about the artists who dominated the Indiana music scene during the 1950s, '60s, '70s, '80s, and '90s. Included are sections devoted to jazz and country and western. For easy reading, the artists are listed alphabetically with their brief biographies.

Goshen's contribution is important since he worked tirelessly to preserve historical data regarding the artists. Many of them are instantly recognizable, but Goshen leaves no one out by focusing on those who may have been "one-hit-wonders," or performed for a short time. Regardless of their lack of national fame, they will now never be forgotten.

Let The Good Times Roll is important for another reason. While New York City, Los Angeles, Memphis, Nashville, and Chicago are normally given credit as hotbeds of rock 'n' roll, jazz, blues, big band, and country and western, this book provides credibility that Indianapolis and the State of Indiana deserve mention as well.

Good, bad or indifferent, Indiana music has for decades held a special place in popular music. *Let The Good Times Roll*, featuring artists from Michael Jackson to John Mellencamp to Hoagy Carmichael to Axl Rose to Wes Montgomery and the Four Freshmen as well as those of lesser renown, is a tribute to the artists that have entertained audiences for more than fifty years! For this we owe a debt of gratitude to Larry Goshen.

Anthony Gourdine, Little Anthony and the Imperials

David Somerville, Lead Singer, The Diamonds

Foreword

Memories
of Indiana are quite special for me. Growing up with my brothers Wes and Monk, I learned that Hoosier hospitality is more than just a catch phrase; it's true. Hoosiers do care about one another, especially when it comes to music.

When I heard that musical historian Larry Goshen and my friend, author Mark Shaw, had completed a book about Indiana music, I was thrilled. So many great artists have their roots in my home state and it's about time someone paid tribute to them.

Of course, Larry and Mark could write an entire book about the Indiana musicians that have played my favorite music – jazz. *Let The Good Times Roll* reminds me of the wonderful memories I have of performing with such Hoosier jazz greats as Pookie Johnson, Slide Hampton, Jimmy Coe, Buddy Parker, Charles Cox, and the grandmaster of them all, Erroll Grandy. How I used to love to hear him play when he visited our home. His talent fascinated Wes, Monk, and me.

I also recall the great clubs that we frequented in Indianapolis. Live performances are the lifeblood of music, and I played at such venues as George's Bar, Henri's, the Sky Club, and the Sunset Lounge. Those clubs were jumping, and the music was smooth and easy. It was a great time in my life.

Besides Jazz, I'm pleased to see that Larry and Mark have included Indiana musicians that focused on pop, rock, and country and western. By dividing the book into sections that features the musicians and their music by decades, they have presented nostalgia at its very best.

I've told people that there was music in my soul from the day I was born. I'm especially pleased to see tribute payed to my brothers, Wes, and Monk. They discovered jazz way ahead of me, but when I was a teenager I began to listen to them. They weren't professionals, but they sounded like it to me. They would get out their guitars and jam together, alternating with one carrying the rhythm, and the other playing solo. It was great fun.

Wes was a special influence. He was a natural and I watched him and listened to the greats of the time, the stylemakers, the creators of the music. They included Duke Ellington, Charlie Parker, Count Basie, Lionel Hampton, Dizzy Gillespie, Erroll Garner, Thelonius Monk, and John Coletrane, among others. I was lucky to meet many of them and hear great stories. But it was Wes that pushed me, encouraged me to learn how to play. He and Monk were terrific brothers and they introduced me to the Indianapolis music scene where so many top musicians were performing.

True inspiration came from Wes when he let me accompany him to a gig in Indianapolis. When the performance was over, I remember him leaving with a good-looking girl on each arm while I carried his guitar. I thought, hey, I want to be the one with the good looking girls!

Learning to play with Wes and Monk in Indianapolis permitted us to travel all over the country. In the early 1960s, we performed at the Ware House in Los Angeles. It was owned by the so-called "Rat-Pack" – Frank Sinatra, Dean Martin, Sammy Davis, Jr., and Peter Lawford. I'll never forget riding down in the elevator to the stage area with none other than well-known actors Caesar Romero and Vincent Price. The audience included them, Sinatra, and other famous move stars. It was an exciting evening, playing for all of them in the smoke-filled club. My brothers and I had come a long way from having been born in the 1100 block of Miley Street in Indianapolis.

Wes' career had taken off in Naptown when he was asked to sub for a musician named Maco, Lionel Hampton's regular guitar player. Maco was a terrific rhythm player, but Wes brought a whole new sound to the group and much more charisma. To show how much Indianapolis and his family meant to him, Wes turned down Lionel's offer to join him on the road.

It was during a set at the famous Sunset Lounge that I first became interested in the vibraphones. Wes was playing that night with the Hampton band, but the highlight for me was when they turned the lights down and featured the vibes on a ballad called Midnight Sun. Those gold bars on top stood out like they were real gold and the sound hooked me. I made up my mind that night that I would own a set of vibes in the near future. It wasn't too long after I got the set and began playing that Jimmy Coe, one of the musicians featured in *Let The Good Times Roll*, called and asked me to accompany him and his band on a southern tour to back up Big Joe Turner. I explained that I couldn't read music, but Jimmy said he would show me the tunes. He did and what an experience playing with Jimmy was for me.

Just as I have been able to recall great memories of my days in Indianapolis, others will be able to do so when they read *Let The Good Times Roll*. I'm honored that I was asked to write the Foreword for the book, and I know it will be a success since it features some of the greatest musicians that ever lived.

Buddy Montgomery

The Montgomery Brothers – Wes, Monk, and Buddy

Author's Note

When I was a kid growing up in the town of Needmore, Indiana, there was no television. But I do remember a radio. My mother would listen to country music. Until age nine, I swallowed a steady diet of Ernest Tubb and Hank Williams.

In 1950, my mother, two brothers and I moved to Indianapolis to be closer to where my father worked. I could finally absorb different styles of music. From age ten until around 13, I was fascinated with Frank Sinatra's "Learnin' The Blues," singer Mindy Carson, and the Four Ace's recording of "Standing On The Corner," the song about watching all the girls go by!

In 1955, rock n' roll just stood-up and kicked me in the ass. Chuck Miller's version of "The House Of Blue Lights," started things, and Bill Haley's "Rock Around The Clock," from the movie, Blackboard Jungle, put me in gear. From that moment, music was my life.

While attending Arsenal Technical High School in Indianapolis, I studied flute and French horn before switching to the drums. I focused on drums after I attended a teen dance and heard my first live band. When the band took their intermission, my friends persuaded me to approach the stage and play the drums. I had never played a set before, never even played the drums, but I found the groove. The kids enjoyed the performance. That surprised many people, including the drummer, who was a little uptight.

Excited, I convinced my parents to buy my first set of drums the next day. Purchased at Arthur's Music Store in Fountain Square, Indianapolis, my dad paid $287 for a Ludwig set. It included a snare and base drum and a 12" Zildjian cymbal. Not much of a set, but was good enough to learn with. I built it up over the years.

In 1957, my first band, a three-piece group, was called The Crowns. It included Chuck Ellis (guitar), Danny Beach (guitar), and yours truly on drums. We played Elvis and Carl Perkins tunes. We performed on several television shows, including Jimmy Mack's "Teens and Tunes."

In 1958, I joined pianist Jimmy Ganzberg. We performed as a duo. Jimmy fascinated fans with his impersonation of Jerry Lee Lewis. In 1959, I became a member of Jerry Lee Williams and the Crowns. We recorded one record on the Solid Gold label. The songs were entitled "Wibcee," and "The Go Tune," both instrumentals. After member changes, we used the name, Sounds of the Crowns. We continued to perform record hops and live stage shows.

In 1959, while performing in Terre Haute, I had the good fortune to appear on stage with singer Jackie DeShannon. Our group handled the sound check for Jackie and we performed on the same show. She was very young, around 16, but her performance was one that I will never forget.

In 1963, I joined the road group, The Five Checks. For two years, we toured the Midwest. Many special moments have occurred since then. Music has always been a special part of my life. I still perform once in a while, but my main interest is to capture the past and present, preserving the music, the singers, the musicians and the entertainers that were so enjoyable.

Music truly does make the world go around. It affects our moods, and adds to everything we do. Can you imagine a film without music surrounding the scenes that make us laugh, make us sigh, or make us cry? Without music, there would be no dancing. Can you imagine that?

The entertainers mentioned in this book deserve an Indiana Musician's Hall of Fame. Until that occurs, I hope this book is a living tribute to their achievements.

Larry Goshen

Book Categories

Segregating artists into various categories for this book was extremely difficult. The question may arise: Why is a particular artist included in a certain category? The answer is that selection was based on when the artist or artists were best known. In some instances, a classification was made due to the start of a music career.

When difficulty is encountered finding an artist or artists, check several categories. Future editions will include additional artists.

The categories include:

THE FANTASTIC FIFTIES
This section is dedicated to entertainers that performed mostly for teenagers during the birth of Rock & Roll and R&B. Many of the artists performed later in their careers in other ventures.

THE SENSATIONAL SIXTIES
This section is based on the artists and music targeted at teens and young adults. Garage bands and musicians that played affected the music of today.

NIGHTCLUBS, BARS, AND MUSIC STARS OF THE SIXTIES
This section features musicians and singers that performed in nightclubs and bars in the Indianapolis area and across the nation in the 1960s.

THE SWELL SEVENTIES
THE EMPHATIC EIGHTIES
THE NAUGHTY NINETIES
These sections include prominent groups that gradually became professional and popular entertainers. The 1990s include jazz groups with pop and rock because some musicians during this era performed in many musical categories.

COUNTRY AND WESTERN GUYS AND GALS
While not a complete roster of Indiana country performers, this section recognizes artists with roots in Indiana.

JAZZMAKERS
Indiana jazz performers deserve a book of their own, but this section highlights several that were notable.

Let the Good Times Roll

The Fantastic Fifties

Let the Good Times Roll

The Fantastic Fifties

The post-World War II America was a melting pot for change. Dwight D. Eisenhower became President in 1953, Senator Joseph McCarthy launched his drive to rid the country of communists a year later, and blacks boycotted segregated city bus lines in Montgomery, Alabama in 1956. By 1959, New York City authorized their city council to investigate the potential for it to become the nation's fifty-first state.

On the cultural scene, *All About Eve* won the Academy Award in 1950. Grace Kelly was a movie star as was Marlon Brando, featured in *A Streetcar Named Desire*. Dr. Seuss wrote *The Cat In The Hat* in 1957. Lillian Hellman penned *Toys In The Attic* three years later.

When the year 1950 dawned, popular songs across America included "If I Knew You Were Comin' I'd Have Baked A Cake," "Mona Lisa," "I've Got The World On A String" and "The Tender Trap." During the decade, such hits as "Hello Young Lovers," "House Of Blue Lights," "The Green Door," "Smoke Gets In Your Eyes," and "Purple People Eater" lit up the charts. Elvis Presley chipped in with "Hound Dog" and "Don't Be Cruel." Bill Haley shouted "Rock Around The Clock" to the delight of his fans.

In Indiana, memorable moments were spent at sock hops and teen dances. The Whiteland Barn was a highlight. Music lovers could stand outside and hear the sounds of a rock drummer beating away. Inside, the stomping feet of the rockers could be felt from the loft above. The Barn was so packed it's a wonder it didn't topple.

Built in the 1930s, the Barn was originally a square dance hall. Around 1957, owner Don Holt hosted the first teen dance. Seventy-five teens (only three were girls) showed up on a Sunday night. But word spread and the dances became a ritual for every teen that could wind their way to Whiteland.

Local disc jockeys "Bouncin' Bill" Baker, Jack Morrow, and Jim Shelton spun the platters. Indiana groups such as the Downbeats, Crowns, and Keetie and the Kats provided live music. In later years, the Barn hosted such international celebrities as Jerry Lee Lewis, Chubby Checker, Duane Eddy, Dee Dee Sharp, Johnny and the Hurricanes, The Kingsmen, the Fireballs, Ray Stevens, Bill Black's Combo, and Conway Twitty, then a rock star. The Barn finally closed in 1962 when rock concerts began to draw teens in droves.

Other popular teen clubs during the late 1950s and early '60s were the Westlake Beach Club and the Indiana Roof. Small community centers such as the First Presbyterian Church (16th and Delaware), Fletcher Place, and Brookside Center were popular venues for music. Groups played anywhere they could find space: shopping centers, swimming pools, during intermission at drive-in theatres. Many drive-in restaurants featured music and DJ's – Merril's Hi-Decker, Al Green's, and Pam's Drive-in. Rock shows were held at the Speedway Theatre and teens danced at the old Wagonwheel.

Besides Bill Baker, Jim Shelton, and Jack Morrow, disc jockeys included Johnny Spring, Hal Fryar, Bernie Herman, Frank Prater, Tom Mathis, Dick Summer, and Easy Gwynn. Bill Baker, a great entertainer and a hilarious comedian, was unique. Many times he dug into his own pocket to pay bands a bit extra. He was also a friend to all – musicians, teens, fans, everyone.

Let the Good Times Roll

The teen bands of the 1950s played rock-a-billy, twangy rock, and basic rock n' roll. Those great sounds should never be forgotten. Many are still classics today. What follows is a tribute to those who played and gained fame, and those who played but did not. Regardless, they all contributed to the enjoyment of music lovers during the **Fantastic Fifties.**

ART ADAMS

Indianapolis-based Art Adams began his music career circa 1959 by playing rhythm guitar and singing with a four-piece country group. This band entertained at picnics, car lots and the country barn in Whiteland. They even performed on local radio shows. Later, in 1959, drums and another guitar were added, and "The Rhythm Knights" was created. While working teen dances with a local television disc jockey named Jim Laythrop, Art and The Rhythm Knights were given a chance to record. In 1960, Art recorded for the Nashville record

company, Cherry Records. He earned attention with his recording of "Indian Joe." He later played the nightclub circuit and performed at the White Front, Playmor and other nightspots in the Indianapolis area. Art's recordings are highly collectable selling for $100 in the United States and $400 to $500 overseas. His recordings include "Rock Crazy Baby/She Don't Live Here No More" (1960), and "Dancin' Doll/ Indian Joe" (1960) on Cherry Records

ART ADAMS (1960)

Let the Good Times Roll

ART ADAMS & THE RHYTHM KNIGHTS

ART ADAMS
KY CURLY
RAY GADBERRY
HAROLD KNIGHT
EDDIE WIEL

*ART ADAMS
& THE RHYTHM KNIGHTS (1960)
Left to right: Roy Robinet – Ray Gadberry
– Eddie Wiel – Harold Knight – Front: Art
Adams*

"BOUNCIN' BILL" BAKER

Born in Tarentum, Pennsylvania, Bill Baker first experienced the world of entertainment at the age of six by singing live on radio station WWSW. Baker moved to Indiana around the age of twenty-five. He made his Hoosier radio debut at station WIOU in Kokomo. Around 1956, Baker was hired by station WIBC in Indianapolis as the announcer for the Burn't Toast and Coffee program. He became the highest rated DJ in Indianapolis history. In 1962, Baker was named by Mirror Magazine, "Disc Jockey of the Year." Baker, an accomplished drummer, is a member of the "Disc Jockey Hall of Fame." In 1964, Baker was master of ceremonies for the first Indiana appearance of The Beatles.

"BOUNCIN' BILL" BAKER

Let the Good Times Roll

BOYD BENNETT

Boyd Bennett, originally from Nashville, Tennessee, moved to Indianapolis in the late 1950s. He purchased the Thunderbird, a local popular nightclub. Boyd signed with Cincinnati's King Records in the mid-1950s. He recorded two hits, "Seventeen," and "My Boy Flat Top." In 1956, Bennett received national attention with "Blue Suede Shoes," recorded on the King Label. Boyd later signed with Mercury Records, and recorded a lesser hit entitled, "Boogie Bear." Boyd Bennett died, June 2, 2002.

BOYD BENNETT (1955)

THE BLUE ANGELS

BUD OSBORNE
BUDDY PARISH
RICHIE SCHATZ
DENIE SMERDEL

Formed in the summer of 1960, the original group was comprised of Denie Smerdel, Bud Osborne, Richie Schatz and Buddy Parish. Members changed through the years. Osborne and Smerdel remained as the nucleus. In September 1963, Osborne entered

THE BLUE ANGELS

college. Greg Galbraith joined the band for a year before it disbanded. Galbraith later moved to Nashville, where he became a well-known studio musician.

THE BLUE JEANS

JOHN BIGGS
PAUL FRENTZ
BOBBY LEE
JIM TITTLE

A teen band formed in 1959.

Let the Good Times Roll

Boyd Bennett & Big Moe

THE BOPPERS

CHARLES ANDERSON
JIMMY ANDERSON
RUDY BARTLETT
JIMMY GUILFORD
TOMAS MITCHELL
BILL MOSLEY

The Boppers were members of several groups formed in the 1950s, including the Four Sounds and the Monograms. Singer Jimmy Guilford became a member of the famous Lamplighters.

THE BOPPERS (1952)
Left to right: Jimmy Anderson – Charles Anderson – Tomas Mitchell – Jimmy Guilford – Rudy Bartlett – Bill Mosley

JIMMY CLENDENING

Indiana-born Jimmy Clendening was a popular singer with teens in the late 1950s. As a featured singer with the popular Keetie & The Kats band, Jimmy recorded "That's the Way," and "Dreamers Romance," a 45 single release on the K-W label.

JIMMY CLENDENING
With KEETIE & THE KATS
Left to right: Dave Ellman – Larry Lee – Jimmy Clendening – Keith Phillips – Norm Shafey

Let the Good Times Roll

JIMMY COE

Although not from Indiana, Indianapolis has been Jimmy Coe's home for more then seventy-five years. He was born in Tompkinsville, Kentucky, March 20, 1921. An established Jazz musician, Coe performed with many great artists, including Freddie Hubbard, J.J. Johnson and Wes Montgomery. In 1953, Jimmy recorded 12 songs for States records. One of the recordings, "After Hours Joint," sold over 300,000 copies. Performing on this recording with Jimmy Coe were James Palmer (piano/organ), Earl "Fox" Walker (drums/talk) and Remo Biondi (violin/guitar). In 1958, Coe recorded a local R&B hit entitled "Wazoo" on the Note label. Collaborators were Henry Cane, Will Scott and Earl "Fox" Walker. Coe's recording of "Cold Jam For Breakfast" (1966) was on the Intro label. His earlier recordings, "I Got It Bad And That Ain't Good" and "Cole Tater" were recorded on King Records under the name of Jimmy Cole.

JIMMY COE ORCHESTRA
Left to right (front): Ray Smith – Vincent Stewart – Jimmy Coe – Sim Graves.
Left to right (back): Eldridge Morrison – Ted Turner – Ernest Griffin – Hillard Duerson – Earl "Fox" Walker

THE CONTEMPORARIES

AL FINNELL JR.
ERMON HUBBARD JR.
AL OFFICER
GERALD "CORKY" RUARK

This band, under the direction of Al Officer, played R&B, pop, and some jazz. Most of their bookings were at college functions and local dance clubs. Two additional members of this group were Rozelle Boyd, a future Indianapolis city counselman, and Freddie Hubbard.

THE CONTEMPORARIES (1954)
Left to right: Al Finnell Jr. – Ermon Hubbard Jr. – Al Officer – Gerald "Corky" Ruark

THE COUNTS

THE COUNTS
Left to right (back): Robert Wesley – Robert Penick – James Lee.
(front): Chester Brown – Robert Young

CHESTER BROWN
JAMES LEE
ROBERT PENICK
ROBERT WESLEY
ROBERT YOUNG

The Counts were formed circa 1952 while students at Crispus Attucks High School in Indianapolis. They formed a bond of friendship that lasted through the 20th Century. Their first recording, "Darling Dear" was released in 1953. It climbed to #6 on the national R&B charts. The group's original name was The Diamonds, but they were required to change when a national act used a similar name. The Counts other recordings include, "Hot Tamales" (1954), "My Dear My Darling" (1954), "Baby, I Want You" (1954), "Let Me Go Lover" (1954), "From This Day On" (1955), "Sally Walker" (1955), "Heartbreaker" (1956), on the Dot label, and "Sweet Names" (1956) on the Note label.

Let the Good Times Roll

THE CROWNS

DANNY BEACH
CHUCK ELLIS
LARRY GOSHEN

The Crowns performed at many teen venues in the Indianapolis area. They appeared on many local radio and television shows in the early 1950s. Around 1959 (after member changes), they recorded under the name of Jerry Lee Williams & The Crowns. Drummer Larry Goshen was the only original member to continue with the Williams group. This photograph of the Crowns was taken 1958 at the Eastgate Shopping Mall in Indianapolis before it was enclosed.

THE CROWNS (1958)
Left to right: Danny Beach – Chuck Ellis – Larry Goshen

THE DAWNBEATS

BOB CARRIE
DICK DONAHUE
DON HERALD
PHIL RAMEY
MORGAN SCHUMACHER

The Indiana-based band, The Dawnbeats, performed in teen clubs such as the Indiana Roof Ballroom. They were a house band that entertained weekends at the popular Whiteland Barn. Featuring guitarist and singer Bob Carrie, the group made one double-sided recording in 1959. The songs were "Drifting" and "Midnight Express" on the AMP label. Morgan Schumacher later performed with rock n' roll artists such as Chuck Berry. After the death of Bill Haley, he became the permanent drummer for the touring band, Bill Haley's Comets.

THE DAWNBEATS (1959)
Left to right: Bob Carrie – Don Harold – Phil Ramey – Morgan Schumacher – Dick Donahue

THE DEB TONES

LINDA HIRT
KAREN LEMASTERS
JULIE WILSON

This singing trio was formed in the late 1950s under the name, The Petticoats. They later changed their name to The Deb Tones, and recorded for RCA Records. The Deb Tones made many personal appearances in Indianapolis including the Jimmy Mack Television show, *Teen Twirl*.

THE DEB TONES (1958)

THE DEB TONES With JIMMY MACK (1958)

Let the Good Times Roll

DANNY DOLLAR (DOWLER)

Danny Dollar was a local singer who possessed a touch of the Elvis sound, and a style and sound of his own. As a teen singer, he excited the girls with his physical actions and artistic voice. Later in his career, he toured the United States and performed with such artists as Bo Diddley and Gregg Allman of the Allman Brothers. In 1967, he recorded "Hello Blues" and "Telling You Like It Is" on the Solid Soul label.

DANNY (DOWLER) DOLLAR (1957)

JACKIE DE SHANNON
JACKIE SHANNON

Originally from Hazel, Kentucky, Jackie DeShannon performed many times in the Indiana area. In 1959, she was popular with her version of Elvis Presley's hit recording, "Trouble." Her first hit, "Faded Love" was released in 1963 on Liberty Records. In 1964, she was the opening act for the Beatles when they performed their first American tour. In May of 1966, she recorded a Burt Bacharach and Hal David song entitled, "What The World Needs Now Is Love." The song was nominated for four Grammies. Many famous artists including Brenda Lee, the Byrds, the Fleetwoods and Kim Carnes have recorded songs DeShannon wrote.

(Left to right) BILL BAKER – DALE WRIGHT – JACKIE DE SHANNON (Live show, Terre Haute, 1959)

JACKIE DE SHANNON

Let the Good Times Roll

THE DOWNBEATS

BOB CARRIE
DON HERALD
MORGAN SCHUMACHER

The forerunner of the popular Dawnbeats band, they re-grouped in 1959 and changed their name to the Dawnbeats. (See Dawnbeats for information.)

THE DOWNBEATS (1957)
Left to right: Morgan Schumacher – Bob Carrie – Don Harold

CHUCK BERRY with drummer MORGAN SCHUMACHER
(Bass player unknown)

THE FASCINATORS

Don Kelley originally formed the Fascinators in the late 1950s. The Terre Haute group was well known for their great singing and fantastic choreography. The Fascinators performed at the popular Indiana Theater in Terre Haute. They attracted a large following at the Whiteland Barn, Indiana Roof and Westlake in Indianapolis. Original members included Lou Corey, Larry Fuqua, Boyd (Popcorn) Johnson, Don Kelley and Jim Carsey. Singer Don Kelley later formed The Swingin' Lads, a popular Las Vegas act. They appeared several times on

Left to right: Larry Fuqua – Lou Corey – Jim Carsey – Boyd (Popcorn) Johnson – Don Kelley. Performing live at intermission for the showing of Elvis Presley's film, King Creole. (Indiana Theatre, Terre Haute, 1958)

the Ed Sullivan and Dean Martin television shows. Kelley also performed with such artists as Tom Jones, Louis Armstrong, the famous Nicholas Brothers, and many others. In the 1980s and 90s, several successful reunion concerts for the Fascinators were held in Terre Haute. Performing for capacity audiences, each show was as professional and exciting as if it were 1959. The group's last concert was performed in August, 1997 in Terre Haute with the Terre Haute Symphony Orchestra under the direction of Orcenith Smith.

Let the Good Times Roll

THE FASCINATORS (1958)
Left to right: Don Kelley – Don Richetta – Jim Calvin – Larry Fuqua (front): Jim Carsey

THE FIVE STARS

Left to right (back): Larry Huffman – Ron Russell – Bill Campbell (front): Boyd (Popcorn) Johnson – Jimmy Bruhn

In 1957, music icon Dick Clark said, "Atom Bomb Baby is destined to be a national hit." That was the year before one of Indianapolis' hottest singing groups – The Five Stars, appeared on American Bandstand. The song, recorded on Dot Records reached the number one spot in Indianapolis, but it never achieved the status Clark predicted. Backing up the group on the recording was Boyd Bennett (of "Seventeen" fame,) and the legendary saxophonist Jimmy Coe. The Five Stars had debuted circa 1957 when Jim Bruhn joined with four other Indy teens, Bill Campbell, Larry Huffman, Ron Russell and Bruce Miller. Boyd "Popcorn" Johnson later replaced Miller. Their first recording was released on Kernel Records and was

later re-released on the national Dot label. Their second recording "Pickin' On The Wrong Chicken," was released in 1958. It earned them a guest appearance on Dick Clark's American Bandstand. On this recording, The Five Stars were backed by members

of the Count Basie Band. Recordings of The Five Stars include "Atom Bomb Baby/You Sweet Little Thing" (1957) Kernel/Dot labels, "Pickin' On The Wrong Chicken/Dreaming" (1958) Note/Hunt labels, "My Paradise/ Friction" (1958) and "Gambling Man/ Am I Wasting My Time" (1958) on the Note label.

THE FIVE STARS (original group)
Left to right (back): Ron Russell – Bill Campbell – Larry Huffman
(front): Jimmy Bruhn – Bruce Miller

Let the Good Times Roll

THE FOUR FRESHMEN

DON BARBOUR
ROSS BARBOUR
BOB FLANIGAN
HAL KRATZCH

Replacements
KEN ERRAIR (1953)
KEN ALBERS (1956)
BILL COMSTOCK (1960)
RAY BROWN (1973)

While attending Indianapolis-based Butler University in 1947, Don and Ross Barbour formed "The Toppers." The group included their cousin Bob Flanigan and good friend Hal Kratzch. Since the Barbours, from Greencastle, and Kratzch, a native of Columbus, were freshman at Butler, they changed the name of the group to "The Four Freshmen." While playing at a nightclub in Dayton, Ohio, the singers were discovered by bandleader Stan Kenton. He arranged a recording contract with Capital Records. The Four Freshmen's recording of "It's a Blue World," became a national hit in 1952. Later recordings such as "Day By Day," "Candy" and their classic, "Graduation Day" were successful in the 1950s. In all, The Freshmen recorded more than 30 albums.

THE FOUR FRESHMEN (1959)

THE FOUR SOUNDS (1959)
Left to right: Bill Harris – Jimmy Scruggs – Jimmy Guilford – Kenny Moore

Let the Good Times Roll

THE FOUR SOUNDS

JIMMY GUILFORD
BILL HARRIS
KENNY MOORE
JIMMY SCRUGGS

The Indiana-based Four Sounds appeared on many top R&B labels, but they never received the recognition they deserve. The Four Sounds recorded for Universal Records, a Detroit label, around 1959. They also recorded on the Tuff label around the same time. In 1961, they released their biggest hit, "Someone To Show Me The Way," on the famous Federal label. Latter in the 1960s, Jimmy Guilford teamed up with singer Jimmy Scruggs and became a popular nightclub act in the Indianapolis area. The Four Sounds recordings include, "Funny Feeling/The Ring"(1959) on Universal Records, a re-release of "The Ring/Peters Gun" (1959) on Tuff Records, and "Someone To Show Me The Way" (1961) on Federal.

THE GALAXIES

Ron Jackson
Larry Parish
Bill Wedsner

JIMMY GANZBERG

Indianapolis-born Jimmy Ganzberg was a graduate of Arsenal Technical High School in Indianapolis. Jimmy played piano at the age of three. During high school, he performed with his own band and made several recordings. Ganzberg attended Indiana University's Jordan Conservatory of Music studying under jazz icon David Baker. His Jerry Lee Lewis style was very popular. On one occasion, he performed on an open-top piano. To the shock of the audience, the hammers from inside flew out over his head. Ganzberg was a great pianist and entertainer, and performed with fantastic showmanship. He later worked his

JIMMY GANZBERG (1957)

Left to right: Edgar Bateman – William Boyd – Jimmy Coe – Jerry Lee Williams – Jimmy Ganzberg (Recording session for Jimmy Ganzberg's, "White Saddle Shoes.")

JIMMY GANZBERG with Jimmy Mack and drummer Larry Goshen. (1957)

way into soul & jazz, and performed with musicians Marden Baker, Glen Douglas and other jazz artists. Jim lives in Madison, Alabama, and continues to perform in that area. His recordings include "Hang Out/JoEllen" (1958), "White Saddle Shoes" (1958), and "Rebel Yell/Twilight and Tears"(1958), with the Crowns band featuring saxophonist Jimmy Coe. All were recorded for the Indianapolis record label, Jet.

LARRY GARDNER

Versatile bassist Larry Gardner (Wazoo) played with many groups including the popular Keetie & The Kats. Larry toured for a short time with The Five Checks and returned to Indianapolis to perform with The Downbeats and Teach & The Tracers. Larry, retired from music, resides in Hiltons, Virginia.

GARY GILLESPIE

Indiana's Gary Gillespie was one of the first Indianapolis teen idols. He was popular in the late 1950s. Gary performed in local teen clubs and enjoyed top billing in most DJ record shows. He appeared with WIBC disc jockey's Jim Shelton, Bill Baker and Jack Morrow. His first recording, Let the Good Times Roll

LARRY (WAZOO) GARDNER (1959)

"Honest I Do/Dancing Girl" (1961), was released on Delta Records. Gillespie later joined the nightclub circuit singing with groups such as The Katalinas and the By Chantz Operation. His last recording was on the BCO label. The songs were "Blue Lover," and "My Sweet Cindy."

GARY GILLESPIE (1958)

HAMPTON SISTERS

The Hampton Sisters, Aletra, Carmalita, Dawn and Virtue represent an historical music family. Born in Middletown, Ohio, they learned to play musical instruments when they were three years old. They traveled the country performing with their parents, Laura and Clarke (Duke) Hampton. While playing in Indianapolis in the late 1930s, the family decided to make Indiana their home. Following World War II, the Hampton Sisters played and performed with the family swing group, the Duke Hampton Band. It included family members Clark Jr. (Duke), Maceo, Marcus, Russell and Slide Hampton.

The band played through the 1950s & 60s and included such musicians as Dick Dickerson, Gene Fowlkes, Pookie Johnson, Sonny Johnson, Sonny Miller, Bill Pennick and Tom Whitted. They performed at the Indianapolis nightclub Steins on North Meridian Street. Later it became Nick & Jerry's. The Hampton Sisters performed with such artists as Nat King Cole and Lionel Hampton, and played in such historical venues as Carnegie Hall and the Apollo Theatre in Harlem. In 1953, the Hampton Sisters recorded at the King Records studio in Cincinnati. The tunes were recorded with the Duke Hampton Orchestra. They made several recording, but only one, "The Push/Please Be Good To Me" on King Records, was released. Accompanying musicians on the recordings included Billy Brooks, Leo Cornett, Russell Hampton, Iid Ferguson, Slide Hampton, Harry Bell, Thomas Badger,

THE HAMPTON SISTERS
Left to right: Dawn – Virtue – Aletra
– Carmalita

DUKE HAMPTON BAND
Left to right (front): Russell Hampton – Carmalita Hampton – Dawn Hampton – Duke Hampton – Thelma Ruth (singer)
Left to right (2nd roll): Slide Hampton – Maceo Hampton – Marcus Hampton
Left to right (back roll): Aletra Hampton – Sonny Johnson.

Aletra Hampton, Carmalita Hampton, Marcus "Lucky" Hampton, Virtue Whitted, Dawn Hampton, Calvin Shields and Duke Hampton. Sisters Aletra and Virtue continue to perform in the Indianapolis area.

RONNIE HAIG (Ron Hege)

A graduate of Arsenal Technical High School in Indianapolis, Ronnie Haig was born March 3, 1939. ABC-Paramount recordings of "Don't You Hear Me Calling Baby," and "Traveler Of Love" (1958), earned Indianapolis native Ronnie Haig an appearance on Dick Clark's American Bandstand. Ronnie toured with the Dick Clark's Caravan of Stars. He performed guitar on many national recordings, including The Five Stars recording of "Atom Bomb Baby" (1957). He later recorded on the Note Label such tunes as "Rocking With The Rhythm And Blues," and "Money Is The Thing Of The Past." In 1996, he recorded his first CD "Branching Out," on the Solid Gold label. Haig was

Let the Good Times Roll

inducted into the Pittsburgh "Roots of Rock & Roll" in 1994, and in 1998 became a member of the "Rock-A-Billy Hall of Fame."

THURSTON HARRIS

Indianapolis artist Thurston Harris first gained fame when he sang with the Lamplighters and the Sharps. After this group released twelve singles, Thurston moved back to Indianapolis to continue his solo recording career. In September 1957, Harris recorded a song that Robert Byrd had written entitled "Little Bitty Pretty One." It became a top 10 hit. Other Harris recordings included "Do What You Did," and "Over and Over," for Aladdin Records. In 1962 and '63, he recorded on the Cub and Dot Records, and in 1964 moved to the Imperial and Reprise label. Thurston Harris died of a heart attack in 1990.

RONNIE HAIG

BOBBY HELMS

While performing on his father's local television show, "Monroe County Jamboree," Bobby Helms was discovered by famed country and western singer Ernest Tubb. This led to an appearance on Tubb's "Midnight Jamboree" and the signing of a national recording contract. Helms gained music immortality with "Jingle Bell Rock," one of the best-selling singles of all time during the Christmas season. He also recorded "My Special Angel," and "Fraulein." Even though Helms was considered a country singer, his songs, recorded for Decca Records, slipped into the pop and rock n' roll charts. Helms died in 1997.

BOBBY HELMS (1958)

CHUCK HIGGINS

Chuck (Charles) Higgins was born on April 17, 1924 in Gary. The son of a preacher that played trombone, Chuck, age ten, loved the trumpet. After leaving Indiana around 1940, Chuck settled in Los Angeles, where he played trumpet in his high school band. Years later, Higgins formed his own band and played the saxophone. In 1953, his biggest hit "Pachuko Hop" was recorded on the Combo label. That permitted Higgins to secure concert bookings with Charlie Parker, Nat 'King' Cole, Johnny Ace and other name artists. Albums recorded by Higgins included "Rock n' Roll Versus Rhythm And Blues" in 1959, and "Motor Head Chuck" in 1979.

JOE HINTON

Born on November 15, 1929 in Evansville, Hinton began his musical career in gospel music. Around the mid-1950s, he moved to Memphis where he recorded with the gospel group, "Spirit Of Memphis." While working for Peacock Records, he switched to R & B music. Joe then recorded "Ladder Of Love" (1958), and "You Know It Ain't Right" (1963) for Back Beat Records. The latter climbed to #20 on the hit charts. In 1964, Hinton's soulful version of the Willie Nelson song, "Funny" reached the #13 spot in the top 100. Hinton continued to record for Back Beat Records before dying of cancer in 1968.

IMPALAS

BILL LUNDWALL
JIM PADGETT
BILL PIERCE
TOM STERGAR
KEITH THOMAS

A Terre Haute band formed in 1959 that toured locally and nationally.

IMPALAS (1959)
Left to right (front): Keith Thomas – Tom Stergar – Bill Pierce
Left to right (back): Jim Padgett – Bill Lundwall

JOHNNY & THE PYRAMIDS

DANNY BEACH
LARRY DEAL
JIMMY (JAMES) ELLIOTT
JOHNNY MOORE

Indianapolis "doo wop" group Johnny

Let the Good Times Roll

& The Pyramids was very popular on the teen scene. They performed at record hops and teen clubs with local disc jockeys. No recordings were made of Johnny & The Pyramids, but one member, Jimmy Elliott, later recorded a 45 single "Sheet Music/Touch and Go," on the American Sound Label.

KEETIE & THE KATS

Perhaps the most popular group working in Indianapolis during the 1950s and '60s was Keetie & The Kats. Keith Phillips (Keetie), was both a talented drummer and showman. He possessed a special gift of gab that helped his band obtain some of the area's best bookings. In addition, Keetie enjoyed success in attracting the most talented musicians to his group. The old saying "Cats Have Nine Lives" fits Keetie & The Kats. Here's why!

JOHNNY & THE PYRAMIDS (1958)
Left to right (back): Larry Deal – Danny Beach – Jimmy Elliott
(front) Johnny Moore

1. The original Keetie & the Kats group formed around 1958. It included Keith Phillips on drums, Dave Ellman on piano and trumpet, Larry Lee on lead guitar, and Bill Rooker on rhythm guitar.
2. In 1959, guitarist Norm Shafey succeeded Bill Rooker.
3. In late 1959, Larry "Wazoo" Gardner, a local bass player, replaced Norm Shafey. Also joining the group was local saxman John Scott and around the same time keyboardist Dave Kellie replaced Dave Ellman.
4. Bass player Bill Settles filled in for Larry Gardner in 1961 and saxophonist Donny Sanders replaced John Scott.
5. In 1962, Larry Lee left the group. The Kats continued to tour as a four-piece ensemble under the name of Bill Black's Combo.
6. Guitarist Gary LeMaster joined the group around 1963 along with clarinetist Bob Snyder (formerly with Tommy Dorsey). The band changed

KEETIE & THE KATS (1960)
Left to right (back): Donny Sanders – Larry Lee – Keith Phillips – Dave Kellie
(front): Bill Settles

Let the Good Times Roll

KEETIE & THE KATS (1958)
Left to right: Larry Lee – Dave Ellman – Keith Phillips – Bill Rooker (Whiteland barn)

LARRY LEE & KEITH PHILLIPS
(1959)

KEETIE & THE KATS (1959)
Left to right: Larry Lee – John Scott – Norm Shafey – Larry Gardner – Dave Kellie
(drums): Keith Phillips

its name to Keetie & The Kasuals and began to play more adult-oriented music, ranging from pop to Dixieland.

7. In 1964, Bob Snyder left the group and saxophonist Pete Funk and trombonist Jerry Woodward (from the Five Chords) were added.

8. In late 1964, the band changed its name to the Keith Phillips VI. Jerry Woodward left the group and Jesse Williams joined.

9. In 1965 or '66, Bruce Waterman and Skip Wagner joined the group. In 1967, The Keith Phillips VI broke up. The members scattered across the country.

Keetie & The Kats played the Whiteland Barn and other popular teen clubs in Indianapolis during the late 1950s and early 60s. Local singers that worked with Keetie's group during this time included Jim Clendening, Jerry Seifert and Dennis Turner. Recordings made by Keetie & The Kats include, "Move Part I & 2" (1960) on K-Records, and "Way Out/Crossties" (1962), on the Huron label.

Let the Good Times Roll

DAVID LERCHEY (THE DEL VIKINGS)

Born in New Albany, Lerchey was baritone singer for the nationally known group, "The Del Vikings." This group became the first successful multi-racial rock n' roll band since Lerchey was white and the other members African American. The group became popular in 1957 with their smash hit, "Come Go With Me." It climbed to number four on the national charts. That was the highest position achieved at the time by a mixed-race group. One of Del-Vikings later recordings, "Whispering Bells," was listed on the Billboard charts at number nine.

BOBBY LEWIS

Bobby Lewis was born in Indianapolis on February 17, 1933. He began his career by selling pots for a traveling Indian. He also sang for a road show called "Bimbo's," and then worked for funnyman Soupy Sales. Lewis' first recording around 1956 was taped in Chicago on the "Parrot" record label. He then recorded "Mumbles Blues" for Spotlight Records. In 1958, Lewis moved to the "Mercury" label, with "Oh! Mr. Somebody." Three years later Lewis, recording for Beltone Records, broke through with his big hit "Tossin' And Turnin'." It was number one for seven weeks, and became the most popular song of the year. Lewis returned to Indianapolis twice, once in 1962 to appear with the Dick Clark Caravan of Stars at the Indiana State Fairgrounds. Later he performed on the bandwagon for the Nixon Administration.

JIMMY MACK

Jimmy Mack was born in Lincoln, Nebraska. He moved to Indianapolis around 1957. He appeared on station WISH with his live Teens 'N Tunes radio show. His wife Peggy co-produced, and the dance program was top-rated. From 1957 until 1963, Jimmy was master of ceremonies for Teen Twirl, a popular television program on the Indianapolis station, WISH. That program featured live teen bands and singers such as the popular American Bandstand. Jimmy Mack later hosted the television series, Bandstand 13, on Indianapolis station WLWI. Mack appeared on other television and radio stations. He performed commercials for such shows as Amos & Andy, the Mouseketeers, and the Annie Oakley Show. Jimmy Mack

Let the Good Times Roll

JIMMY MACK (1958)
Live on WISH television program, Teen Twirl.

JIMMY MACK (1958)

lives in the Indianapolis area where he is a successful photographer.

LONNIE MACK

Lonnie Mack was born in Harrison, Indiana in 1941. He began playing professionally at early age by working in clubs and roadhouses around Indiana, Ohio and Kentucky. Famous for his Flying V Gibson guitar, Mack recorded many songs for King and Federal Records in Cincinnati. He played with R&B artists such as Hank Ballard, Freddie King and James Brown. In 1963, Lonnie recorded an instrumental version of Chuck Berry's hit, "Memphis" on Fraternity Records. It rose to number five on the charts. Other Mack recordings were "Wham!" "Where There's A Will There's A Way" and "Chicken Pickin." Lonnie Mack also made an appearance on the Door's "Morrison Hotel" album. He appeared with such major artists as Stevie Ray Vaughn, Bob Dylan, Mick Jagger and Paul Simon. Lonnie Mack is still playing nationally as a guitarist and entertainer.

Let the Good Times Roll

LONNIE MACK BAND (1963)
(Names not in order) Wayne Bullock – Truman Fields – Ron Grayson – Marv Lieberman – Irv
Russotto (far right): Lonnie Mack

ND WITNESSES

GARY DRAPER
DON ELLIS
DOUG METCIK
DOUG STERNS
JIM TUTTEROW
DENNY WILSON

Guitarist/leader Doug Sterns formed this group in the late 1950s. Sterns later re-united this group in the 1980s to perform in the nightclub circuit. The group was called Witness.

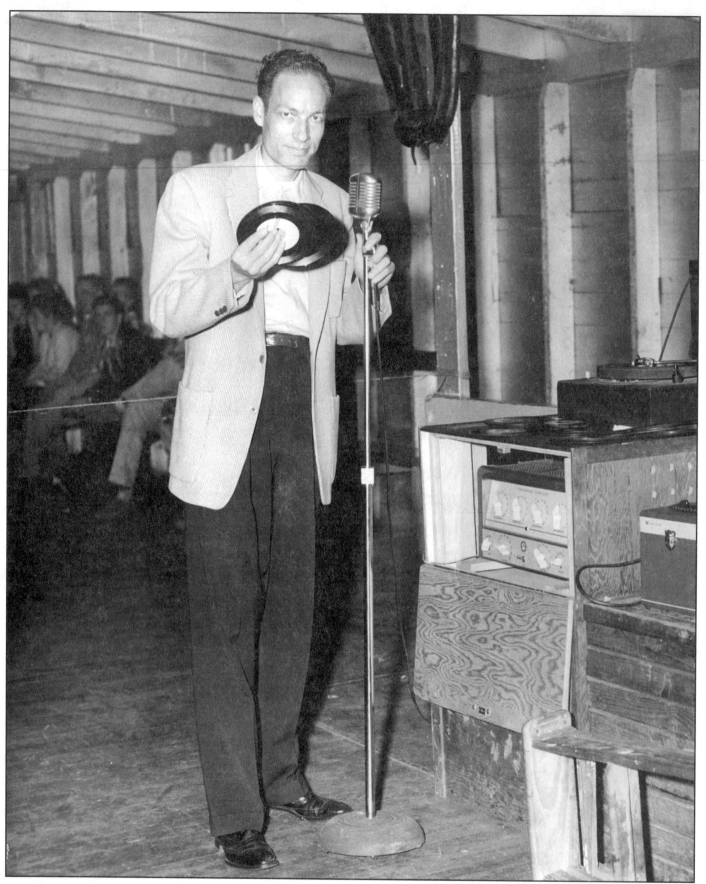

JACK MORROW (1950s)
WIBC disc Jockey
(The Whiteland Barn)

Let the Good Times Roll

THE PLAYBOYS

JERRY JAQUESS
GARY MC KIERN
BILL ROBERTS
JIM SPILKER
BILL VALE
GENE WHEELER

This 1950s Indianapolis teen band was one of the several groups who used the Playboy name.

NOONEY (EVERETT) RICKETT

Nooney Rickett was born in Hazard, Kentucky. In the late 1950s, he lived in Indianapolis and attended Arsenal Technical High School. He recorded "Heaven on Earth/Trying to Forget" (1960), on MGM Records, and "Bye Bye Love/In the Swim" (1964), on 20th Century Fox. He later recorded on the Dimension, IT, and the Capitol labels. Nooney also made a guest appearance in a beach movie with Frankie Avalon and Annette Funicello. In 1958, Nooney could be seen at the Arsenal Grill across from Tech High School slouched in a booth, strumming his guitar.

NOONEY (EVERETT) RICKETT

THE ROCKIN TONES

CARL JUNIOR CAMPBELL
DARREL WAYNE CHENOWITH
JIMMY CHENOWITH
RAY (LITTLE RAY) CHENOWITH
GLEN WESTERFIELD

ROOKER & THE ROCKERS

BILL ROOKER
GUY TARRENTS
DEAN WAGNER

THE RHYTHM ROCKERS

JOHNNY BENNETT
GEORGE CARTER
CHARLIE (BROWN) CLARK
JIM CROSSEN
FRED LAWSON
JACK SCOTT

ROOKER & THE ROCKERS (1959)
Left to right: Guy Tarrents – Bill Rooker
– Dean Wagner

JERRY SEIFERT

Indiana-born Jerry Seifert recorded his only local hit, "Dirty White Bucks/Never Baby Never" (1958) on Note Records. ABC Paramount recording artist Ronnie Haig wrote both songs. In the mid-1980s, Jerry released another single, "Rockin Fifties/My Love Just Ain't Getting Through" on the Sundial label.

THE SHADES

JIM LORMAN
JIM SLACK
JOHN TABOR

JERRY SEIFERT (1958)

TROY SHONDELL

Born in Fort Wayne, Troy Shondell was an accomplished musician who attended Valparaiso University. While majoring in music in 1961, he recorded and produced a song entitled, "This Time." He released it on his own label, "Gold Crest." Liberty Records learned of the song and Shondell

Let the Good Times Roll

recorded it on their label. It zoomed to success climbing to number six on the top Billboard 100 and remained there for twelve weeks.

THE SHOWMEN

WALT REED
DOUG STERNS
JERRY THOMPSON
JIM TUTTEROW
BUDDY VAN OSDOL
GIL WORK

Other members were:
JACK ALDRICH
STEVE SMITH
DAVE THOMPSON

THE SHOWMEN (1957)

THE SOUNDS OF THE CROWNS

JOHN BENNETT
LARRY GOSHEN
JACK SCOTT
BILL STEWART
GARY THAXTON
DICK WALTERS

The Indianapolis-based band Sounds of the Crowns never recorded under this name. They had released an earlier single under the name of Jerry Lee Williams & The Crowns, recorded on the Solid Gold label. This group was quite popular with the teens, playing record hops with disc jockey's "Bouncin' Bill" Baker and Jim

THE CROWNS
(1958) Live at the Westlake Beach Club.

Let the Good Times Roll   35

Shelton. They also appeared at Westlake and the Whiteland Barn.

LARRY GOSHEN (1958)

THE SPANIELS

OPAL CORTNEY JR
GERALD GREGORY
JAMES "POOKIE" HUDSON
WILLIS C. JACKSON
ERNEST WARREN
Later members were JAMES COCHRAN, DONALD PORTER, CARL RAINGE and LESTER WILLIAMS.

This singing group from Gary first performed together at Roosevelt High School around 1953. Their initial recording, "Baby It's You," was performed on the Chance label, later known as Vee Jay Records. The Spaniels were the first group to be signed by the Vee Jay label. Their first hit occurred in 1954 with "Goodnite Sweetheart, Goodnite." Other recordings included, "You Painted Pictures" (1955), "You Gave Me Peace Of Mind" (1956), "Everyone's Laughing" (1957), "Stormy Weather" (1958), and "I Know" (1960).

THE TURBANS

BOB BERNARD
CHARENCE DORSEY
TONY GOODRICH
HILTON HUDSON
HERMAN LEWIS

This group was formed in 1957. It was re-formed by singer Bob Bernard and re-titled the Monograms. In the 1960s, The Monograms became one of the top soul acts in Indiana. (See Monograms, Nightclub section)

Let the Good Times Roll

JERRY LEE WILLIAMS & THE CROWNS

LARRY GOSHEN
BILL STEWART
GARY THAXTON
DICK WALTERS
JERRY LEE WILLIAMS

Formed in 1959, and together for only a short time, this group recorded "The Go Tune/Wibcee" (1959), on Solid Gold Records. "Wibcee" became a popular recording, but short-lived because of its title and the fact that it only played on WIBC Radio. Due to a disagreement between Williams and the other members, he was replaced by guitarist Jack Scott. The group became The Sounds of The Crowns.

JERRY LEE WILLIAMS
& THE CROWNS (1958)
Left to right: Larry Goshen – Bill Stewart – Jerry Williams – Dick Walters – Gary Thaxton

TOMMY WILLS

Tommy Wills was born in Middletown, Ohio. He moved to Indianapolis in 1971. Wills learned the guitar at the age of eight. After entering junior high, he switched to saxophone. Wills made several recordings in the mid-1950s.

Some have become collector's items. Wills recorded on the Club Miami label. In 1954, he recorded a song entitled, "Let Em Roll" featuring singer Marti Maes. That recording is valued in the $250 price range and sought after in the collectors market. In 1961, Wills recorded under the name of The Tomcats and released a single on Terry Records. In 1963, he hit the national charts with his instrumental recording of "Man With A Horn." It was released on Gregory Records. Wills has toured the United States and Canada, performing everything from country and swing to rock n' roll. After moving to Indianapolis, he performed on the Holiday Inn circuit. In the 1980s, he directed the Ted Weems Orchestra. Wills later directed the Eddy Howard Orchestra. In 1989, he toured with Bill Haley's Comets. Wills released

TOMMY WILLS

two CDs "Swingin' The Blues," a recording with the big band sound, and the Christmas CD, "Happy Holidays."

DALE WRIGHT

Dale Wright, an Ohio native, performed with some of Indiana's top bands including Keetie & the Kats, the Dawnbeats and the Crowns. His recording of "She's Neat" (1958) on Fraternity Records climbed to the #39 position on the Billboard charts. Wright made guest appearances on American Bandstand and the Merv Griffin Show. He also performed as a character actor for the national network series of The Rifleman.

AL (ALPHONSO) YOUNG

DALE WRIGHT (1959)

Alphonso Young was born in Louisville, Kentucky. He moved to Indianapolis in 1959. A guitarist, he performed with the Presidents and appeared at George's Place on Indiana Avenue. In

1962, Young left for Clarksville to join guitarist Jimi Hendrix. They formed a group entitled the King Casuals. In 1963, Hendrix moved the group to Nashville and Al returned to Indianapolis. Young continued to perform with the Presidents and other local bands. Members of the Presidents include Louis Cochran, Harold Elery, Leroy Massey, and Mr. "T," Howard O'Brook, Phillip Slaughter and Al Young.

AL (ALPHONSO) YOUNG

JIMI HENDRIX & AL YOUNG
(1950s)

AMOS ARTHUR (1950s)
Proprietor of Arthur's Music Store, Fountain Square, Indianapolis.

Let the Good Times Roll

The Sensational Sixties

Let the Good Times Roll

The Sensational Sixties

When John F. Kennedy was elected President of the United States in 1960, the country was as optimistic as his smile. Three years later, he would be assassinated. A year prior to his death, Cuba nearly caused a world war by permitting the Soviet Union to base missiles on its shores. When Nikita Khrushchev backed down, the world was saved from potential extinction.

As the decade progressed, civil rights became the call of the wild. Riots in the south were met with determination by Dr. Martin Luther King and his followers. An assassin's bullet in 1968 ended his crusade. That year John Kennedy's brother, Robert, a presidential aspirant, suffered the same fate at the hands of Sirhan Sirhan.

By the end of the decade, the nation had witnessed the surreal musical happening at Woodstock and the amazing achievement of Neil Armstrong landing on the moon. The Chicago Seven trial was held. Abbie Hoffman and company became front page news.

Cultural events besides Woodstock included the penning of *One Flew Over The Cuckoo's Nest* by Ken Kesey. An art exhibit by pop artist Andy Warhol featured his Campbell's Soup can, and the first James Bond film, *Goldfinger* highlighted the New York film scene.

The Sensational Sixties marked a revolution in modern music. The decade featured the evolution, among others, of the Beatles, the Rolling Stones, the Beach Boys, and crooner Roy Orbison. The Temptations, the Four Tops, and Ruby and the Romantics were favorites. Ed Sullivan's television program was a must-see.

Popular songs of the'60s included, "Cathy's Clown, "The Twist," "Go Away Little Girl," "Last Train To Clarksville," and "Aquarius." The Beatles entertained the world with "Hard Day's Night," "Eleanor Rigby," "I Want To Hold Your Hand," and many others.

Indiana-born or Indiana-based musicians played their part in the rock revolution, but they also contributed to the soul and jazz scene. Young people in the '60s congregated at the Flame Club, the House of Sounds, the Pink Panther, the Speckled Axe, the Tiger-A-Go-Go, and Party Time. Jim Shelton and Bill Baker continued to be popular disc jockeys as did Tom Mathis, Reb Porter, and Jay Reynolds.

Teenagers kept up to date with developments in the rock arena through monthly publications. The most popular was *Teen Tempo*, an Indianapolis publication that provided local rock groups with visibility.

In every nook and cranny, "Garage bands" emerged during the '60s. That connotation was unfortunate since the bands were creative and popular. Many gained fame despite their being laughed at for rehearsing in garages.

Across Indiana, the blend of rock, soul, and jazz provided a perfect mix for music lovers. The musicians and groups that follow contributed to a time when the listening was easy during **The Sensational Sixties**.

THE AQUANAUTS

DAN BOTNICH
STEVE HARDING
TOM HARDING
LEE MORRELL
WALLY MURPHY

This Indianapolis band released two singles, "Rumble on the Docks" and "High Divin'" (1963), on Safari Records.

THE BACKDOOR MEN

FRED HOSTETTER
STEVE KREIDER
DEAN TAGGART

From Elkhart, Indiana, this group recorded one 45, "Evil/Corinna" (1969), on the Fujimo label.

THE BOYS NEXT DOOR

JIM ADAMS
SKEET BUSHOR
STEVE DRYBREAD
JIM KOSS
STEVE LESTER

Originally called the Four Wheels, this Indianapolis group changed their name around 1965 to The Boys Next Door. They produced several recordings, "Why Be Proud/ Suddenly She Was Gone" (1965), on Soma Records, "There Is No Great

BOYS NEXT DOOR (1965)

Sin/I Could See Me Dancing With You" (1966), on Cameo, and "The Wildest Christmas/Christmas Kiss" (1966), on the Bad label.

ROY CHANEY

Bass player Roy Chaney was born in Indianapolis in 1948. He performed with the psychedelic group, The Count Five. This group recorded "Psychotic

Let the Good Times Roll

Reaction" (1966), on the Double Shot label. The recording reached the number five spot on the Billboard charts.

CHANCES 'R

STEVE FOSSEN
ALLEN KIRSCH
RON RUTJES
CHRIS SKILLMAN
LARRY STREUBER

This band hailed from Chesterton. They produced one recording, "I'll Have You Crying/Winds and Sea" (1965) on the Quill label.

THE CHECKMATES, LTD.

SONNY CHARLES
MARVIN SMITH
ROBERT STEVENS
HARVEY TREES
WILLIAM VAN BUSKIRK

The Checkmates were formed in 1957 in Fort Wayne. They were one of the first racially mixed ensembles, and made their first recording on the Chicago based I.R.P. label in 1963. In 1969, they recorded "Black Pearl" on the A&M label. It climbed to number thirteen on the Billboard charts and remained in the top 100 for ten weeks. After a short, inactive period during the early 1970s, leader Sony Charles re-formed the group. It became successful in Las Vegas as a show band. This group performs in Las Vegas, and has won several awards for "Best Lounge Act."

THE CHECKMATES, LTD.
Left to right: Bill Van Buskirk – Sonny Charles – Marvin Smith – Harvey Trees – Bobby Stevens

THE CHOSEN FEW

THE CHOSEN FEW (1967)
Left to right: Steve Nephew – John Cascella – Carl Storie- Jack
(Happy Jack) Hamilton – Richie Berman – Haji Baba

DAVE BARNES
DAVE BENNETT
JOHN CASCELLA
JACK HAMILTON
CARL STORIE

This band recorded several singles on the Denim label in the mid-1960s, and one LP, "The Chosen Few" (1969), on RCA. Around 1972, they formed a group called Limousine, and recorded one self-titled album on the GSF label. Less then a year later, they created the popular group, The Faith Band. The original members of this group (shown in the 1967 photo) included Haji Baba, Richie Berman and Steve Nephew.

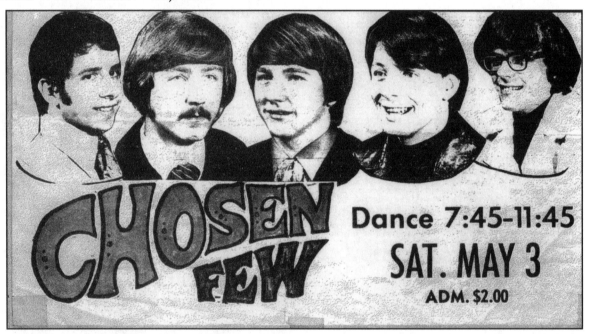

THE CIRKIT

SCOTT GLEMSIECKE
DAVE GOLDMAN
BRUCE HAINEY
ROD HANSEN
MIKE RICHARDS
JIM SHINDELL

Let the Good Times Roll

This Michigan City-based group recorded one single "Yesterday We Laughed/I Was Wrong" (1967), on Unicorn Records.

COVEN

JINX DAWSON
GREG OSBORNE
STEVE ROSS
DAVE WILKERSON

In 1968, the Indianapolis group Coven recorded their first album, "Witchcraft" for Mercury Records. Since the name "Coven" denoted an assembly of witches, the group's music was banned in Detroit. In the late 1970s, Coven hit the charts with "One Tin Soldier" from the movie soundtrack of Billy Jack. They recorded two other albums under the Coven name, "Coven" on MGM Records in 1971, and "Blood On The Snow" on Buddah in 1974. Other members of the Coven group were John Hobbs, David Larman and Chris Neilsen.

COVEN (1968)
Left to right: Dave Wilkerson – Jinx Dawson – Steve Ross – Greg (Oz) Osborne

THE DAWN FIVE

STEVE BENHAM
DAVE DUNNE
DAVE McKOWN
GREG NICOLOFF
MIKE NICOLOFF

The Dawn Five from Indianapolis opened for such national acts as The Turtles and Sonny & Cher. They recorded one single "A Necessary Evil/ Mike's Bag" (1965), on the Bee Gee label.

THE DAWN FIVE

THE ENDD

LARRY ANDERSON
RUSS SANDERS

This La Porte group recorded several singles in the mid-1960s. They included: "So Sad/Emancipation" (1965), "Project Blue/Out Of My Hands" (1966), "Don't It Make You Feel Like Crying/Gonna Send You Back To Your Mother" (1966), and "Come On In To My World/This Is The Zoo, Plus Two" (1966). All were recorded on the Seascape label.

THE FOUR WHEELS

JIM ADAMS
SKEET BUSHOR
STEVE DRYBREAD
JIM KOSS
STEVE LESTER

The Four Wheels preceded the popular Indianapolis group, The Boys Next Door. They recorded one single, "Central High Playmate/Cold 45" (1964), on the Soma label.

DENISE L. GRISSOM

Indianapolis-born Denise Grissom began performing as a vocalist at the age of thirteen. After graduating from Shortridge High School, Denise continued entertaining in the 1960s by working with the all-female group, The Pearls. She later performed with many national and regional acts, including recording artist Stevie Wonder. Denise performs in the Indianapolis area and continues to work the jazz circuit with drummer Dick Dickinson.

THE HEAVY

LARRY INGLE
PHIL THOMPSON
FRANKIE WATTERS
JEFF WILLIAMS

This Kokomo-based group was known for their wild clothes and equally wild stage antics. Guitarist and singer Phil Thompson performs under the name of Phil T. Blues. He has made several recordings. (See 1990s).

THE HEAVY (1968)
Left to right: Larry Ingle – Phil Thompson
– Frankie Watters – Jeff Williams

Let the Good Times Roll

HICKORY WIND

ALAN JONES
MIKE McGUYER
BOBBY STREHL

This Evansville group recorded one album entitled, "Hickory Wind" (1969) on the Gigantic record label. Only 100 copies were pressed making this record highly collectable. Price range from $500 to $1000 per album. This band preceded the B. F. Trike band. They recorded an album for RCA in 1971 that was never released.

THE HIGHLIGHTERS

RICHARD "BOOLA" BALL
JAMES BOONE
JAMES BRANTLEY
JAMES "PORKCHOP" EDWARDS
CLIFFORD PALMER
(Later members)
JAMES BELL
DEWAYNE GARVIN

The Highlighters were formed in the early 1960s. They re-formed around 1968 with singer James Bell and drummer Dewayne (Funky Buzzard) Garvin. This band played the local nightclub circuit. In 1969, they recorded the regional hit, "Poppin' Popcorn," on the Rojam label. They later recorded a James Bell original entitled, "The Funky 16 Corners," released on the Three Diamonds label. The Highlighters members changed, but they made five more recordings before disbanding. They recorded on the Three Diamonds, Chess and Lulu labels.

THE HIGHLIGHTERS

HIM HER & THEM

BOB DAWSON
JINX DAWSON
STEVE FARBER
GREG JOHNSON
DAVID LARMAN
GREG OSBORNE

Formed in 1964 in Indianapolis, two members of this group (Jinx Dawson & Greg Osborne) later became part of Coven. (See Coven, 1960s)

THE IDLE FEW

RON BENNETH
RON KNOOP
DAN McLEAN
PAUL ROMINE
RICK WEBSTER

Originally entitled the Kings Men (1958), they changed their name to The Idle Few. The group performed with such artists as the Beach Boys, the Byrds, the Supremes, and Bobby Goldsboro. They recorded "Another World /Farmer John" (1966) on Suma, and the single, "Letter to Santa/ Splishin & Splashin" (1967).

THE IDLE FEW (1962)

Let the Good Times Roll

THE JACKSON FIVE

JACKSON FIVE (JACKSONS)

JACKIE JACKSON
JERMAINE JACKSON
MARLON JACKSON
MICHAEL JACKSON
TITO JACKSON

The Jackson brothers were born in Gary, Indiana. Their father Joe, a guitarist with his own R&B band, the "Falcons," provided musical training. Michael was not an original member of the group, the Jackson Family Singers. It consisted of brothers Jackie, Tito, and Jermaine. Michael and brother Marlon joined to form "The Jackson Five." The group first started performing in clubs around 1962. Their first recording was on the Indiana based label, Steeltown. They auditioned for Motown in 1968, and made their first recording, "I Want You Back," a year later. It was the fastest selling record in the company's history. After many successful recordings with Motown, the contract expired in 1975 and The Jackson Five signed with EPIC Records. After losing a lawsuit filed by Motown regarding the rights to the name "Jackson Five," they became known as the "Jacksons."

ROYAL JONES AND THE DUKES

GARY JONES
GENE JONES
KEITH KILMER
MIKE KISER
JAY PURVIS
SKIP WALTERS
DAVE WORKMAN

An early 1960s band from Goshen that recorded on Fujimo and a Chicago based label entitled Signett.

JOYS OF LIFE

JIM ALBRECHT
CRAIG GARDENER
CORKY KIRK
DANNY McMULLIN
JEFF McMULLIN
JEFF MILLS

In 1967, this Indianapolis group recorded, "Good Times Are Over/ Descent," a 45 single on Columbia

JOYS OF LIFE (1967)
Left to right (front): Jeff Mills – Corky Kirk – Danny Mc Mullin
(middle): Craig Gardener – Jim Albrecht
(top): Jeff McMullin

Let the Good Times Roll

Records. Recording on a National label was a great achievement for a local group, but the song was not a national success. Bill Overman, a local producer who helped many other bands achieve local success, produced this recording. In the 1990s, musician Jim Albrecht opened a recording studio. He performed with such groups as Small Talk, Trinia & The Gypsies, and many others.

THE KNIGHTSMEN

DARRELL BALL
KARL HINKLE
GARY IRWIN
DAVID LEE
DONALD LEE
ROB McCOY
TOM REA
MARK TRIBBY

THE KNIGHTSMEN

Formed in 1965, this Indianapolis band recorded one single, "Gimme Some Kinda Sign/Let Love Come Between Us." The Knightsmen disbanded around 1968. Singer Karl Hinkle later became a member of the popular Wright Brothers band. (See Wright Brothers, 1970s)

THE LORDS OF LONDON

HARRY CANGANY
MARTY LAMBERT
MIKE LEKSE
RICHIE MEDVESCEK
FRANK WECHSLER

Formed in1965, this Indiana band made two recordings, "Broken Heart Of C.O.D./Sit Down And Dance" (1965), on the Domain label, and "Time Waits For No One/Cornflakes And Ice Cream" (1966) on Decca.

THE LOST SOULS

DANNY DAIN
CHARLEY HINKLE
JOHN MOORE
PHIL THOMPSON
DAVE TRUEBLOOD

This Kokomo band was formed in 1967. They performed across Indiana.

THE McCOYS

RANDY HOBBS
BOBBIE PETERSON
RANDY ZEHRINGER
RICK ZEHRINGER

This Indiana and Ohio-based group was formed in Union City, Indiana in 1962. The McCoys became famous three years later with their Bang Records recording of "Hang On Sloopy." Another top ten entry was a sound-alike version of Sloopy titled, "Fever." The group disbanded in 1969. Later guitarist Rick Zehringer (second from left) changed his last name to Derringer. In 1973, he joined the popular Edgar Winters band.

THE McCOYS (1965)
Left to right: Randy Zehringer – Rick Zehringer – (DJ) Bob Berry – Bob Peterson – Randy Hobbs

ME AND THEM GUYS

MARTY BAKER
ROD KERSEY
STEVE MICHAEL
STEVE PRITCHARD
CRAIG TERRY

High school students from Greencastle formed this band. The group was popular in local teen clubs and performed regularly at Purdue University. They recorded one single in 1965, "I Love Her So/Somethin' Else" on the Grette label.

KEITH MURPHY & DAZE

 JERRY ASHER
JOHN ASHER
PHIL FOSNOUGH
KEITH MURPHY
BILL SHEARER

KEITH MURPHY & DAZE
Left to right (top): Phil Fosnough – Jerry Asher – John Asher
Left to right (bottom): Bill Shearer – Keith Murphy

Let the Good Times Roll

This rock group from the Marion area was formed in 1964. It released one single on the King label. It was one of the last recordings pressed on King before the death of owner Sid Nathan. Due to his death, only 100 copies were produced making this recording valuable for record collectors. Valued in the $1000 price range is "Slightly Reminiscent Of Her/Dirty Ol' Sam" (1968) on King. Singer and guitarist Keith Murphy also recorded an earlier local hit "Cindy Lou/Little Loved one" (1963) on the Stacy label. That was under the name of Keith O'Conner. It also featured the group The Torkays.

THE OUTSIDERS

DAN HAILEY
MIKE RAY
ROB SWEENY
WAYNE WILSON

This Indianapolis band claimed to be associated with the national recording artists, The Outsiders. They recorded "Time Won't Let Me" in 1966. Even though this group toured under the Outsiders name, none of these members performed on the original recording.

RIVIERAS

PAUL DENNERT
MARTY FORTSON
DOUG GEAN
OTTO NUSS
JOE PENNELL

This band, originally called The Playmates, did not originate in California, as some might assume, but in South Bend, Indiana. The Rivieras achieved much commercial success in the 1960s with their hit recording of "California Sun." It climbed to the number five spot on the Billboard charts. They later recorded two lesser hits, "Let's Have A Party" and "Rockin' Robin." In 1964, the Rivieras recorded two LP's, "Campus Party" for Riviera (701) and "Let's Have A Party" on the USA (102) label.

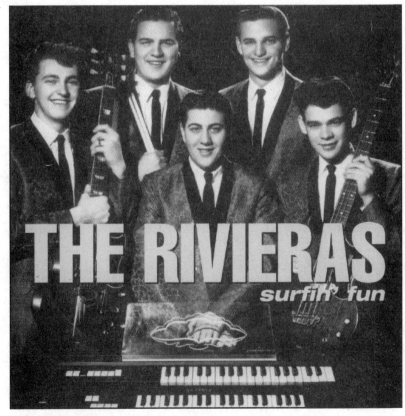

THE RIVIERAS

Front Row—Tom Mathis, Chuck Browning, Bill Donnella, Jay Reynolds, Bob Lyons. Back Row—T. J. Byers, Dick Saint, Reb Porter, Don Lancer, Ron Jackson, Ron Hofer.

WIFE DISC JOCKEY'S

REB PORTER
(DJ for WIFE radio station)

Let the Good Times Roll

THE SENTIMENTALS

HENRY HINCH
JOSEPHINE TERRELL

This classic Motown-style duo was formed in Indianapolis in 1962. Touring the United States, The Sentimentals opened for such artists as Chuck Jackson,

THE SENTIMENTALS (1968)
Josephine Terrell – Henry Hinch

Patti LaBelle & The Blue Belles, Little Anthony & The Imperials, Martha & The Vandellas, and The Marvelettes. They performed from 1962 through 1970, and recorded one single "I Know You To Well/Now Is Here" (1970), on the Naptown label.

THE SANGRALADS

PHIL ARMSTRONG
MIKE BIDDLE
AARON BURNELL
RICK INGLE

The Sangralads were formed in 1966 at the Sangralea Valley Boys Home at Logansport. The group made exclusive tours of the United States, and performed locally at clubs such as Indiana Beach. They also appeared on the Jim Gerard Show. Their recordings include, "Mary's Kid/Think Of What You're Saying" (1968), and "Quasar 45/There Must Be Light" (1969), on the Whap Record label.

THE SHY ONES

BONNIE MC DOWELL
ROBIN MC DOWELL
BARB GABRIEL
CAROL BUCKOSKI
JEANNE SCHULLER
SANDY GAY

This all-female band was formed in Indianapolis in 1968. The Shy Ones were quite popular on the college circuit performing at many local fraternities. During the Vietnam War, they entertained at Fort Harrison and performed for the troops overseas. The two McDowell sisters later formed the popular Indiana show group, Five Easy Pieces. (See Five Easy Pieces 1970s)

THE SHY ONES (1968)

Let the Good Times Roll

SIR WINSTON & THE COMMONS

DON BASORE
HERBIE CRAWFORD
RONNIE MATELIC
JOHNNY MEDVESCEK
JOE STOUT

This Indiana group was very popular with teenagers. In 1966, they opened for the Byrds at the Indianapolis Coliseum. They recorded two singles, "Come Back Again/We're Gonna Love" (1965) on Soma Records, and "Not The Spirit Of India/One Last Chance" (1967), on Nauseating Butterfly.

SOUNDS UNLIMITED

PHIL BRANDT
STEVE FOSTER
KEN MAHLKE
WAYNE WILSON

The Sounds Unlimited was very popular in the mid-1960s. They played in teen clubs such as Westlake, Indiana Roof, Flame Club, the Pink Panther and the Whiteland Barn. They opened for national groups like the McCoys, Byrds and Mitch Ryder and the Detroit Wheels. Two later members, Terry Talbot and John Talbot formed the 1970s rock group, Mason Profit. The Sounds Unlimited recorded one single. "A Girl As Sweet As You" (1967), on the Dunwich label.

THE TIKIS

BOB FOLGER
DAVE WEBSTER
RICK WORKMAN
PAT WO

A band formed in Syracuse around 1966.

SOUNDS UNLIMITED (1966)

THE TORKAYS

FRANK AGUILAR
JIM AGUILAR
ROCKY HALL
KEITH MURPHY (O'CONNER)
RICHIE NIVERSON

THE TORKAYS
Left to right: Keith Murphy – Jim Aguilar – Rocky Hall – Frank Aguilar

This popular group from Marion and Sweetser performed in the early 1960s at Indiana Beach and other local teen dances. Their release of "Karate" (1963) was the premiere recording of any martial arts theme. "Karate/I Don't Like It" was released on the Stacy label. The Torkays featured Keith O'conner. He also recorded "Cindy Lou/Little Loved One" on the Stacy label. It was released around the same time.

JUNIOR WALKER (AUTRY DeWALT)

Saxophonist Junior Walker, born Autry DeWalt in Blythesville, Arkansas, spent his teenage years at a high school in South Bend. In Indiana, he coined the name Junior Walker and formed his first band, "The Jumping Jacks." After graduating from high school, Junior played in local jazz and R&B clubs. In the late 1950s, he moved to Battle Creek, Michigan. There he formed Junior Walker & The All Stars and began his successful recording career. Walker was one of Motown's most popular artists. He recorded many charted hits. Some of Junior Walker's most popular recordings include "Shotgun" (1965), "Shake and Fingerpop" (1965), "How Sweet It Is (to be loved by you)" (1966) and his first vocal recording "What Does It Take (to win your love)" (1969). Junior Walker died of cancer in Battle Creek, on November 25, 1995.

THE XL'S

TED BENNETH
G. C. EGY
BILL EVANS
TIM FERGUSON
GREG FUNK

This mid-1960s band was from Terre Haute.

OTHER 1960 NOTABLES

ASTRONAUTS
BILLY DAY
BECKI HOLLAND
DICK DEWAYNE
DICK SUMMER
DICK YORK
DOUG STAUCH
FABULOUS JOKERS
HARRY MAGINITY
JAN SANDERS
JIM & DAN BOWLIN
JOHN HARDING
KAPRIS
MIKE CLARK
RICK FORTUNE
RON BONHAM
RUNNER WHITTEN
SHADOWS OF SOUND
STEVE BAKER
THE CARDINALS
THE CHORDELLS
THE ILLUSIONS
THE IMPACTS
THE JIANTS
THE JUVENILES
THE NOBLEMEN
THE NOCTURNES
THE RAMRODS
THE REFLECTIONS
THE ROYAL VIKINGS
THE UNTOUCHABLES
THE VENDETTAS
THE WILD THINGS
TINY VEE
VEGAS
WALTER "ARKIE" BITTLE
YOUNG SET

Let the Good Times Roll

Nightclubs. Bars.
and
Music Stars of the Sixties

Let the Good Times Roll

Nightclubs, Bars, and Music Stars of the Sixties

There's

something special about a darkened room, the lighted stage, and the moment when a musical act is introduced to wild applause causing the heartbeat to flutter. Nightclubs and bars are the melting pot of music where fans and musicians alike gather to meet, greet, and enjoy live music.

During the 1960s, Indiana featured a plethora of mystical venues to the delight of those that believe live music is better, or at least as good as sex. They included The Embers, the Towne House, and the Carousel. Others were Nick & Jerrys, Dan-T Supper Club, the Holyoke, Tic Toc and the Rail Club. It was later known as the Peppermint Lounge.

Great jazz and soul clubs included the Pink Poodle, where Jimmy Smith and Arthur Prysock performed, and the Barrington Lounge. It featured the Jimmy Coe Trio with Melvin Rhyne performing on the B-3 organ, and Sonny Johnson on drums. At the Holyoke, the sounds of Billy Day, Wayne Cochran and the immortal Buddy Rich filtered through the smoke-filled room. Other musicians of note include:

Let the Good Times Roll

THE ACCENTS

DICK DONAHUE
RON RUSSELL
VINCE SANDERS

The Accents were a very popular trio from the Indianapolis area. They performed on the nightclub circuit and were noted for their smooth harmony. They recorded four albums, "Full Spectrum" on Forward Records, "Yesterday Today, and a Touch of Tomorrow" on RCA and "Next Bus South" and "Two Sides of the Accents," on Entertainer Records.

THE ACCENTS
Left to right: Ron Russell – Dick Donahue
– Vince Sanders

ANDY ANDERSON & THE JETS
Left to right (back row): Ralph Coverstone – Andy Anderson – Don Higgs (front roll):
(unidentified) – Jimmy Ganzberg

MARDEN BAKER QUINTET

MARDEN BAKER
LARRY GOSHEN
JACK SCOTT
BILL STEWART
GARY THAXTON

This quintet performed a jazz-rock sound and entertained in many of Indianapolis' top nightspots. This group was originally entitled, The Sounds Of The Crowns. They changed their name to better fit the nightclub circuit. The group performed floorshows backing up such acts as the Cavaliers, Monograms and Gary Wells. Headlining the group was tenor saxophonist Marden Baker. Later members included Jim Ganzberg and Ron Loschky.

MARDEN BAKER QUINTET #2 (1961)
Left to right: Larry Goshen – Rondo Loschky – Gary Thaxton – Jimmy Ganzberg – Marden Baker

THE BLUE TONES

MICKEY KIRKPATRICK
MYRON MURRY
DANNY ORNUNG
JIMMY THEROS

The Blue Tones were a road group that appeared in Indianapolis in the early 1960s. The members were exceptional musicians on the nightclub circuit. When the band eventually left Indianapolis, guitarist/singer Jimmy Theros joined another group and made Indianapolis his home

THE BLUE TONES (1961)
From bottom to top: Danny Ornung – Myron Murry – Mickey Kirkpatrick – Jimmy Theros

Let the Good Times Roll

BY/COUNTS

MEL JAMES
ROBBIE McVEY
RICHIE MARTIN
JIM THEROS

This band performed in the local nightclub circuit. It featured former Blue Tones singer Jim Theros, and drummer/vocalist Mel James.

THE CAVALIERS

LARRY ALLEN
MIKE SHANE

The Indianapolis-based Cavaliers performed at teen concerts and local nightclubs. They entertained at the Whiteland Barn and the Westlake Beach Club. On the nightclub circuit, they performed in such clubs as the Dan T and Nick & Jerry's. The Cavaliers was Indiana's version of Dean Martin and Jerry Lewis. Their showmanship and harmony earned them great popularity.

BY/COUNTS (1963)
Left to right: Richie Martin – Robbie McVey – Jim Theros - Mel James

THE CAVALIERS (1960)
Larry Allen – Mike Shane

Let the Good Times Roll   69

RAY CHURCHMAN

Let the Good Times Roll

RAY CHURCHMAN

Ray Churchman was born in Connersville and moved to Indianapolis when he was fourteen. After taking lessons from drummer Melvin Miller and graduating from Shortridge High School, he joined the Army and performed with the U. S. Army Band until 1945. Ray performed at The Embers and The B & B nightclub and such venues as Clowes Hall and the Fox Burlesque. He backed up artists like Zoot Sims, Pete Fountain, Mel Torme, Ernie Ford, Wayne Newton and Buddy Greco. In 1958, Churchman was a staff musician for Channel 13 and performed for the George Willeford and Don Melvoin Shows. In 1977, Indiana Governor Bowen and Indianapolis Mayor Richard Hudnut honored Churchman for his musical services to the city. Ray was married to the popular television and radio personality Carolyn Churchman and often performed on her shows.

THE CLASSMEN

JIM BRUHN
DICK DONAHUE
DAVE ELLMAN
MEL JAMES

This Indianapolis group was derived from some of Indiana's past bands. Singer Jim Bruhn was a member of The Five Stars. Dick Donahue played with the Dawnbeats and Dave Ellman evolved from Keetie & The Kats. The Classmen were known for their vocal harmony. They also performed comic routines.

Let the Good Times Roll

THE CRACKERJACKS

GARY BEDELL
LARRY GOSHEN
PAUL HUTCHINSON
JACK SCOTT
GENE WITTHERHOLT

The Crackerjacks were re-formed from the Indiana touring band, The Five Checks. Although most members of the rock group were from Indianapolis, many of their engagements were in Illinois and Missouri. The Crackerjacks disbanded in 1964. Bedell, Goshen, Hutchinson and Scott returned to perform in Indianapolis.

THE CRACKERJACKS (1963)
Left to right (top): Gene Witherholt – Gary Bedell – Jack Scott
(bottom): Larry Goshen – Paul Hutchinson

BOBBY DARK

Indianapolis-based singer Bobby Dark was popular in the late 1960s and early 1970s. He performed at some of Indy's top nightspots such as The Hungry Eye and The Red Frog. Dark occasionally performed with the group Chain Reaction. It featured his sister Darlene Dowler.

BOBBY DARK & DARLENE DOWLER

Let the Good Times Roll   73

THE DAWNBEATS (2)

DAVE ELLMAN
LARRY (WAZOO) GARDNER
LARRY LEE
TONY NASSER
MORGAN SCHUMACHER

Morgan Schumacher, founding member of the original Dawnbeats, formed this group in 1960. They performed on the nightclub circuit in the Indianapolis area. Saxophonist Tony Nasser lives in Cincinnati and is a regular member of the popular oldies group, Hot Wax. Drummer Morgan Schumacher performs for Haley's Comets, a group derived from music legend Bill Haley's old band.

THE DAWNBEATS #2
(1960)
Left to right: Tony Nasser – Morgan Schumacher – Larry Lee – Dave Ellman – Larry Gardner

DEL & THE ROAD RUNNERS

DELBERT BAILEY
JIM BOWERS
RAMON LOPEZ

This country/rock band worked the Indianapolis bar circuit, performing with different members. Later

DEL & THE ROADRUNNERS
Left to right: Eddie Green – Delbert Bailey – Dallas Reynolds – Kenny Lee Kernodle – Al Ficklin

members included Furman Brown, Jerry Collins, Al Ficklin, Eddie Green, Willie Phillips and Dallas Reynolds. Drummer Ramon Lopez played percussion for the Stan Kenton Orchestra.

DEL & THE ROAD RUNNERS (1961)
Left to right: Delbert Bailey – Ramon Lopez – Jim Bowers

DEL & THE ROAD RUNNERS
(1964)
Left to right: Furman Brown – Delbert Bailey
– Willy (Phillips) Jones – Jim Bowers
(On stage at the Pla-mor tavern)

Left to right: Bill Stewart (Crowns) – Delbert
Bailey (Road Runners) – Charlie Rich
(On stage at the Starlite Paladium)

Let the Good Times Roll

THE PACESETTERS (1962)
Left to right: John Ness – Duke Demaree – Danny Ornung – Myron Murry – Larry Dowd (not in photograph)

DUKE DEMAREE

Indianapolis-born Duke Demaree took his first drum lesson at age four from his father John. He was drummer for the famous Charlie Davis Band. Demaree played drums during his high school years. After graduating, he continued to pursue music as a career. He performed with many local bands and in 1962 toured with the group, The Pacesetters. This band performed with such artists as Troy Shondell, Rusty Draper, and Little Anthony & The Imperials. In 1965, Duke joined the group Scarlets that included Gary Belaire, Dino Patterson, Boyd Rogers, Bunis Rogers and Wes Charles. With this group Demaree doubled on trombone and drums. He later returned to Indianapolis and continued to perform with bands in the local nightclub scene.

Let the Good Times Roll

DANNY DOLLAR & THE COINS

TOMMY ADAMS
DANNY DOLLAR
RALPH MEYERS
GARY McCARTY
DON WILSON

This nightclub group featured popular 1950s singer Danny Dollar. The Coins performed at the Whitefront Tavern and other clubs around the Indianapolis area.

DANNY DOLLAR & THE COINS
Left to right: Don Wilson – Gary McCarty – Danny Dollar – Tommy Adams – Ralph Meyers

THE DOMINOS

PAUL GRAY
HARVEY GROVE
FRED LAWSON
RONDO LOSCHKY
BILL ROBERTS

The Dominoes performed on the Indianapolis bar scene. They backed up many musical acts including The Monograms.

THE DUKES

CHUCK BEST
JIM HICKMAN
JIM SONDAY
DICK WALTERS

The Dukes, formed in 1961, performed in the Indianapolis area. They began by playing teen dances with DJ Dick Summer. The Dukes became popular in the twist craze era by performing at the Rail Club, an Indianapolis hot spot. At the Rail Club, the Dukes filled the room nightly with a capacity audience. They were so successful the club changed its name to the Peppermint Lounge. It attracted Chubby Checker and Joey Dee and

THE DUKES
Left to right (top): Jim Hickman – Chuck Best – Dick Walters (front); Jim Sonday

the Starliters. After the Dukes left, the club owner obtained rights to the band name. The band was forced to use The Original Dukes as a new title. The Dukes changed personal and later included Marden Baker, Gary Bedell, Bob Crabtree, Al Officer and Fred Williams.

ELLMAN-JAMES DUO

DAVE ELLMAN
MEL JAMES

This duo was formed around 1967. They entertained on the Indianapolis nightclub circuit. Mel James (Melvin Walden-James) later became a jazz journalist and has written for many popular publications.

THE EPICS

ART ADAMS
HARVEY GROVE
PAUL HUTCHINSON
JACK SCOTT
GARY THAXTON

This group from Indianapolis worked the local bar scene and featured popular rock-a-billy singer Art Adams. The Epics performed in such clubs as the Fortress and the Hungry Eye. Later members include Bill Stewart and Guy Tarrents.

THE EPICS
Left to right: Paul Hutchinson – Guy Tarrents – Art Adams – Gary Thaxton – Bill Stewart

THE EPICS (1965)
Left to right: Harvey Grove – Paul Hutchinson – Art Adams – Gary Thaxton – Jack Scott

Let the Good Times Roll

THE FIVE CHECKS

DELBERT BAILEY
BOB EDWARDS
LARRY GOSHEN
PAUL HUTCHINSON
BILL ROBERTS

This group, formed in 1963, performed in nightclubs throughout the Midwest. Top vocals and comedy made this band popular at such venues as the Club Idaho in Terre Haute, The Decatur Lounge in Decatur, Illinois and Nick & Jerry's in Indianapolis. When members changed, the band became known as The Crackerjacks.

THE FIVE CHECKS (1963)
Left to right (top): Paul Hutchinson – Delbert Bailey – Bob Edwards (bottom): Larry Goshen – Bill Roberts

THE FIVE CHORDS

ROD DERKS
HARRY KELLETT
JACK LEWIS
ARLEY PRICE
JERRY WOODWARD

This show group from Terre Haute was very popular in the Indianapolis area. They performed at such clubs as the Boom Boom Room and the Pink Poodle. They recorded "Red Wine/I Dream of Jeanie" (1960) on the CUCA label, and "I Need Your Loving/Bedelia Brown" (1961) on SOMA. In 1962 they released a live album on the Boom Label entitled, "The Five Chords Live at the Boom Boom Room." Two earlier members of the group were Glenn Pharris and Byron Small.

THE FIVE CHORDS (1962)

Let the Good Times Roll

THE FIRST IMPRESSION

DAL BAKER
DAVE ELLMAN
MELVIN (MEL) JAMES

The First Impression, from Indianapolis, included former members of many other groups. They included Keetie & The Kats, The Classmen, Ellman-James Duo and the By/Counts. With their refreshing sound of harmony, The First Impression proved to be very popular in the nightclub scene.

THE FIRST IMPRESSION
Left to right: Dave Ellman – Dal Baker – Melvin (Mel) James

FLO GARVIN

Flo Garvin was born in Indianapolis. She was performing at age sixteen on

FLO GARVIN (1960)

the famous Indiana Avenue. In 1952, Garvin made her first recording on the King label. Her original song "I'm On The Outside Looking In" and "Let Me Keep You Warm," featured legendary saxophonist Jimmy Coe. In the late 1950s, she hosted her own television show "Sentimental Journey," on station WFBM. In 1999, Flo Garvin was presented The Jazz Hall of Fame Award from the Indianapolis Jazz Foundation.

GILBERT (GIL) GORDON

Gilbert Gordon was born in Indianapolis. He attended Harry E. Wood High School. Raised in a musical family, Gilbert studied guitar at age twelve and later became an accomplished pianist. He toured with

Let the Good Times Roll

singer Eddie Cash and performed at the Flamingo and MGM Grand Hotel in Las Vegas. In Indianapolis, Gordon has played keyboard with The Suzanne Prince Band, Jimmy Guilford and the Groove Brothers, Tommy Wills, singer Ronnie Haig, and many others.

SUZANNE PRINCE BAND
Left to right: Steve Kennedy – Suzanne Prince – Debbie Campbell – Gilbert Gordon – Larry Lobdell – Carol McKeeman – Sam Oliver. Recorded one album, "Rusty Nails & Promises."

JIMMY GUILFORD

Singer Jimmy Guilford started his musical career at an early age by tap-dancing on street corners for pennies. In the 1950s, he performed with the group the Boppers. Later, he joined the Twilighters, Lamplighters, the Four Sounds and the Monograms. Guilford performed a duo with singer Jimmy Scruggs, and later formed the groups Three Way Street and The Groove Brothers. In the 1990s, Guilford performed regularly at the American Cabaret Theatre and appeared in the productions of Summer Lovin' and Streetcorner Harmony. Guilford's recordings include "Misery Street/ I Want To Be Your Baby" on the Detroit label, Wheelsville, "Too Late To Cry/No Body Loves Me" on Thelma Records, and "Heart Breaker/I Wanna Be Your Baby" on the Solid Hit label.

JIMMY GUILFORD

HOOK, LINE, AND SINKER

EVA JOE
DENVER LEE
TONY LITTLE
DANNY STAFFORD

This Indianapolis nightclub act entertained around Indiana from the 1960s through the 1990s. Featuring singer and drummer Eva Jo, they recorded two albums "Doin It Again," and "Because We Love You," on the Frogg label.

INNER CIRCLE

LARRY BURCH
JOHN HURST
LARRY LEE
GUY TARRENTS

This band, formed around 1967, toured throughout the Midwest. Indianapolis native Larry Lee was a former member of Keetie & The Kats.

INNER CIRCLE (1967)

JESS & THE JOKERS

BOB BROWN
FURMAN BROWN
JESS COLBURN
DAVE HALL
JERRY HALL
LARRY SCOTT
CHUCK WALLACE
REX WAMSLEY

From the Indianapolis area, this band was formed in the early 1960s. The Jokers were mainly a four or five piece group, but had many member changes. The above is the all-around list of members who made this group popular.

JESS AND THE JOKERS (1961)
Left to right: Larry Scott – Jess Colburn – Rex Wamsley

Let the Good Times Roll

THE JEWELS

BILL COOPER
BILL FLIEHMAN
PAUL HUTCHINSON
GARY LE MASTER

The Jewels were formed in 1959 in Huntington, West Virginia. During a road tour through Indianapolis in 1960, they were booked at the downtown nightclub, Nick & Jerry's. After playing that club off and on for a few years, two members of the Jewels made Indianapolis their home. Saxophonist Paul Hutchinson met his wife Darlene at Nick & Jerry's. After his marriage, Paul continued to perform and live in the Indianapolis area. Paul performed with the late Bobby Darrin, The Five Checks, Art Adams and many others. Guitarist/

THE JEWELS (1960)
Live at the Indiana Roof Ballroom.

THE JEWELS (1961)
Left to right: Bill Cooper – Bill Fliehman – Paul Hutchinson – Gary Le Master
On stage at the Stables Nightclub, Anderson, Indiana.

singer Gary LeMaster, a Coal Grove, Ohio native, continued to live and perform in the Indianapolis area. Gary joined the popular Indianapolis band Keetie & The Kasuals. Later, he became a member of the Bobby Rey band, The Hollywood Argyles. In 1969, Gary settled in Las Vegas and played various casinos. He became entertainment director for several hotels and casinos. LeMaster performed at the California Hotel, Sams Town and the Stardust. He met his wife Valerie (also a performer) in Las Vegas. In 1986, Gary became a permanent member of the legendary group the Sons of the Pioneers. He continues to perform with this group across the United States.

THE SONS OF THE PIONEERS
Gary Le Master is second from left (sitting). Back (middle) Sunny Spencer, original member of the Sons Of The Pioneers.

JIMMY & THE EXCEPTIONS

DELBERT BAILEY
JIMMY BOWERS
WILLIE PHILLIPS
GUY TARRENTS

This Indianapolis bar band was formed around 1966. It featured popular singers Delbert Bailey and Jimmy Bowers. Other members were Willie Phillips on keyboard and former drummer of Rooker & The Rockers, Guy Tarrents.

KATALINAS

DICK NEAT
RONNIE SCHROCK
GIL WORK

This group was formed in 1963. They performed in the Indianapolis bar circuit. The band later featured the popular 1950s teen singer Gary Gillespie.

JIMMY & THE EXCEPTIONS
Left to right: Jimmy Bowers – Guy Tarrents – Willie Phillips – Delbert Bailey

Let the Good Times Roll

KEETIE & THE KASUALS

DAVE KELLIE
GARY LeMASTER
KEITH PHILLIPS
BILL SETTLES
DONNY SANDERS

Formerly Keetie & the Kats, this group performed on the Indianapolis nightclub scene. They appeared at such clubs as Nick & Jerry's and the Lemon Twist Lounge, and later toured throughout the Midwest. A later member was musician Bob Snyder of Danville, Indiana who was formerly with the Tommy Dorsey Orchestra. Keith Phillips later purchased a restaurant in California, Gary LeMasters joined the Sons of the Pioneers and Donny Sanders became a popular studio musician in Nashville, recording for Barbara Mandrell and Lee Greenwood.

ORLY KNUTSON TRIO

GLEN DOUGLAS
JIMMY GANZBERG
ORLY KNUTSON

This trio performed the Indianapolis nightclub circuit in the late 1960s and early 1970s. The group featured radio personality Orly Knutson, pianist Jimmy Ganzberg, and popular saxophonist Glen Douglas.

ORLY KNUTSON TRIO
Left to right: Glen Douglas – Orly Knutson – Jimmy Ganzberg

TOMMY LAM

Indianapolis singer Tommy Lam began performing in the late 1950s and continued through the 1960s and 1970s. Tommy fronted his own band through this period. He recorded two singles. "Speed Limit" (1958) on Nabor Records and "Blue Willow" (1959), on the Randall label. The recording of "Speed Limit" has become highly collectable. It is valued in the $250 price range.

TOMMY LAM

Let the Good Times Roll

KENNY LEE & THE ROYALS

JERRY COLLINS
PAUL GRAY
EDDIE GREEN
KENNY LEE KERNOLDE
LARRY GOSHEN

This group, formed around 1962, performed variety shows and appeared at the popular Boom Boom Room in Indianapolis. The Royals featured singer/guitarist Kenny Lee, saxophonist Jerry Collins and keyboardist Paul Gray. Drummer Larry Goshen, who replaced Eddie Green, later became a member of the road group The Five Checks.

JIMMY McDANIELS

Indianapolis musician Jimmy McDaniels is well known for his striking piano arrangements and his stylish vocals. Also an accomplished saxophonist,

Left to right: Jimmy McDanies – Pete Funk. Jam Session (1963)

Let the Good Times Roll

Jimmy performed and conducted for such artists as June Christy, Nat "King" Cole, Rosemary Clooney and Mel Torme. For two years he hosted a radio show on station WSMJ. In 1969, Jimmy recorded for the JMCA label, a self-titled album "Jimmy McDaniels." Jimmy lives in Indianapolis and performs in local nightclubs and the popular Jazz Fest.

THE MONOGRAMS

CHARLIE ANDERSON
BOB BERNARD
BOB (CHICO) PENICK
JOHN VARDIMAN

The Monograms were formed in 1959 in Indianapolis. The combination of friendship and showmanship made this an unforgettable group. The Monograms performed in such clubs as Nick & Jerry's, Minardo's, Starlite Paladium, the Mad Pad, Rail Club and the Hungry Eye. Their last performance was June 14, 1986 at the

THE MONOGRAMS (1963)
Top to bottom: Charlie Anderson – Bob Bernard – Bob (Chico) Penick – John Vardiman

Indy's Heart of Rock n' Roll Reunion. Even though Charlie Anderson was ill, they produced a fantastic performance. Charlie passed away just a few months later. Two other members that performed with the group were George Black and Jimmy Guilford.

THE MONOGRAMS
Top to bottom: Bob Bernard – Bob (Chico) Penick – John Vardiman – George Black

MARY MOSS

Mary Moss was born in Louisville, Kentucky. She moved to Indianapolis in 1958. Her first local engagement occurred at the Thunderbird Nightclub in Fountain Square with recording artist Boyd Bennett. Moss later performed at The Embers, the B&B Lounge, the Pink Poodle and the LaRue's Supper Club. In the 1960s, she performed in Chicago at the Playboy Club, and continued to work the popular Playboy circuit. She also performed as half of the 1950s and 60s nightclub duo King and Mary. Mary continues to perform at the Jazz Kitchen, Jazz Fest and other venues. She has produced several variety shows at the Walker Theatre entitled Les Beaux Art au Feminin! This show featured all female entertainers and was subtitled Women Simply Kickin' It!

MARY MOSS

THE ORIGINAL DUKES

CHUCK BEST
JIM HICKMAN
RICHIE MARTIN
JIM SONDAY

This group was formed in the mid-1960s. They were former members of the Dukes. Forced to change their name due to a nightclub conflict (See Dukes, this section) this band continued to perform at the Lemon Twist and other local clubs. Other members included Dick Walters and Fred Williams.

THE ORIGINAL DUKES (1964)
Left to right: Richie Martin – Chuck Best
– Jim Sonday – Jim Hickman

Let the Good Times Roll

KING AND MARY

Let the Good Times Roll   89

THE ORIGINAL DUKES
Left to right: Fred Williams – Jim Hickman – Dick Walters

THE KEITH PHILLIPS VI

PETE DUQUESNE
DAVE KELLIE
KEITH PHILLIPS
BILL SETTLES
SKIP WAGNER
BRUCE WATERMAN

This band was formed in the mid-1960s. It was the last of the Keetie and the Kats clan. Three members of this group, Dave Kellie, Keith Phillips and Bill Settles were from the Indianapolis area. The Keith Phillips VI performed at Al Hirt's Club in New Orleans, the Beachcomber in Boston and the Sheraton in Puerto Rico. They appeared on national television with such artists as Al Hirt and Mike Douglas.

THE KEITH PHILLIPS VI

Let the Good Times Roll

SALT & PEPPER

BILL BOGBY
DAN HAILEY

The original Salt & Pepper was formed around 1962. It consisted of Bill Bogby and Bill Lynch. In the 1960s, Dan Hailey (formerly with the Outsiders) joined Bogby to form the new Salt & Pepper. This popular duo performed in Indianapolis as such clubs as the Hollyoke and the Hungry Eye.

SCREAMING JIMMY

Screaming Jimmy (James Churchwell) was a popular soul singer in the Indianapolis area in the early 1960s. He performed in local nightclubs and was an occasional singer with Del & The Roadrunners. This band performed regularly at the Fountain Square Tavern in Indianapolis.

SALT & PEPPER (1969)
Bill Bogby – Dan Hailey

SCREAMING JIMMY (1963)
Left to right: Ramon Lopez – Screaming Jimmy (James Churchwell) – Delbert Bailey – Jim Bowers

THE SPORTSMEN

RONDO LOSCHKY
LARRY GOSHEN
BILL ROBERTS
JOHN SCOTT

The Sportsmen was a top-forty band from Indianapolis that worked the local bar scene. Formed in 1964, they played the popular go-go clubs and performed in such places as the Madison Lounge, Rat Fink Room and the Stardust Show Lounge. This group was together through the 1960s before disbanding around 1970.

THE SPORTSMEN (1964)
Left to right: Bill Roberts – Larry Goshen – John Scott – Rondo Loschky

THE SWINGIN' LADS

JIM BRUHN
RON CARROLL
JIM CARSEY
DON KELLEY
BILL LYNCH
MANNY PARIS

The Swingin' Lads consisted of Don Kelley, former member of Terre Haute's popular teen group, the Fascinators,

THE SWINGIN' LADS
Left to right (top): Jim Bruhn – Bill Lynch – Ron Carroll – Don Kelley
(bottom): Manny Paris
Photograph taken with Las Vegas show girls. Second girl from top left with Bill Lynch is actress Goldie Hawn.

SWINGIN' LADS
Left to right: Frank Gorshin – Ron Carroll – Manny Paris – Don Kelley – Jim Dale (Bruhn)

Let the Good Times Roll

THE SWINGIN' LADS (1966)
Left to right (top): Bill Lynch – Ron Carroll (bottom): Manny Paris – Don Kelley – Jim Bruhn

SWINGIN' LADS
Left to right: Ron Carroll – Don Kelley – Ed Sullivan – Jim Dale (Bruhn)

Left to right: Ron Carroll – Tom Jones – Don Kelley – Jimmy Dale

SWINGIN' LADS
Left to right: Don Kelley – Louis Armstrong – Ron Carroll

and Jim Bruhn former member of the Indianapolis group, The Five Stars. Other members included Ron Carroll, Bill Lynch and Manny Paris. This fantastic show group attracted substantial attention by using powerful dance routines, smooth vocals, and exciting instrumentals. Touring as one of the top entertaining acts in the United States, they performed at show clubs in Las Vegas, Reno and Lake Tahoe. They appeared with such artists as Louis Armstrong, Judy Garland, Tom Jones and the Nicholas Brothers, to name a few. Television appearances include the Dean Martin Show and the Ed Sullivan Show (six times).

TEACH & THE TRACERS

LARRY (WAZOO) GARDNER
MORGAN (FURGIE) SCHUMACHER
JIMMY THEROS
TEACH THEROS

This Indianapolis bar band performed in the late1960s. It featured husband/wife duo Jimmy and Teach Theros,

TEACH & THE TRACERS (1969)
Left to right: Morgan Schumacher – Jimmy Theros –Larry Gardner – (front) Teach Theros

Let the Good Times Roll

ex-Downbeats drummer Morgan Schumacher, and ex-Keetie & The Kats bass player, Wazoo.

THE TRAVELLS

JACKIE ASHER
EDDIE (LITTLE EDDIE) JEFFERS
EUGENE SMITH
KENNETH SMITH

This band from Indianapolis was fronted by singer/guitarist Eugene Smith. The Travells were a long-lasting group that changed members like the change of seasons. Other members include Gary Hamilton, Paul Jackson, Gary Jacobsen, Dave Jones, Ronald Khert, and Tom Spencer.

THE TRAVELLS (1968)
Left to right: Kenneth Smith – Eugene Smith – Eddie (Little Eddie) Jeffers – (front) Jackie Asher

TUTTLE & THE SHELLS

GLEN DOUGLAS
JIMMY GANZBERG
GARY McKIERNAN
MIKE TUTTLE

This quartet from Indianapolis performed a mixture of pop and jazz. The Shells included saxophonist Glen Douglas and popular keyboardist Jimmy Ganzberg. They played the local club circuit and performed a long engagement at the west Sixteenth Street pub called the Whitefront.

TUTTLE & THE SHELLS
Left to right: Jimmy Ganzberg – Mike Tuttle – Glen Douglas – Gary McKiernan

EDDIE WALKER & THE DEMONS

GEORGE ABELL
 LARRY (WAZOO) GARDNER
GENE ROBINSON
MORGAN SCHUMACHER
EDDIE WALKER

EDDIE WALKER & THE DEMONS (1963)
Left to right: Gene Robinson – George Able – Eddie Walker – Larry Gardner – Morgan (Furgie) Schumacher

The Demons from Indianapolis performed in the local nightclub circuit. Featured singer Eddie Walker recorded two singles, "Twistin' Your Life Away" (1963) on the Keet label, and "I Don't Need You Anymore" on Mew Records.

STEP WHARTON

Step Wharton was a popular lounge pianist/singer who performed in the Indianapolis area in the 1950s and 60s. One of his most popular engagements was at the downtown night- spot, the Sherwood Pub.

STEP WHARTON

Even though the bands had many sub-titles, the name Dean Wolfe will always be remembered on the local nightclub circuit.

DEAN WOLFE

& THE WOLFE PACK
& THE RED MEN
& THE SECOND CHAPTER

Dean Wolfe performed in the Indianapolis area through the 1960s.

DEAN WOLFE

Let the Good Times Roll

The Swell Seventies

Let the Good Times Roll

The Swell Seventies

The era of the 1970s began as America bombed Vietcong supply routes in Cambodia. The war spread to Laos with no end in sight. The U.S. punished one of its own when Lt. William Calley was convicted of premeditated murder for his actions at the Mylai massacre.

In 1972, Richard M. Nixon was inaugurated as President. Watergate proved his downfall and he resigned. Vice-president, Spiro Agnew was disgraced as well. In 1976, Jimmy Carter and Gerald Ford debated the fate of America. The voters chose the Georgia governor to lead the nation.

By 1972, *Fiddler On The Roof* became the longest running Broadway show in history. In 1973, Indiana-born Kurt Vonnegut, Jr. wrote his finest novel, *Breakfast of Champions*. Francis Ford Coppola added his version of the history of the Mafia with the *Godfather* classics. In 1977, the world mourned the loss of singer Bing Crosby.

As the nation coped with the Vietnam War, music during the 1970s reflected a country stretching for an identity. Perhaps the R&B song by Timmy Thomas, "Why Can't We Live Together?" was symbolic of the attitude.

Burt Bacharach began the decade with the hit tune, "Raindrops Keep Falling On My Head," from the film *Butch Cassidy and the Sundance Kid,* starring Paul Newman and Robert Redford. Other songs of note included "Maggie May" by Rod Stewart, the Rolling Stones' "Brown Sugar," "My Sweet Lord," "A Horse With No Name," and "Me And Bobby McGee."

Indiana's version of '70s music produced a plethora of stars. They included The Faith Band, John Hiatt, Jubal, Roadmaster, David Lee Roth of Van Halen, and John (Cougar) Mellencamp. As the decade roared to a close, Disco became the fad as John Travolta lit up the screen in *Saturday Night Fever.* Clubs across Indiana began to play the upbeat music to the delight of fans.

Soul music flourished in Indiana. Groups such as Black Magic, Fresh, and Manchild were popular. A young kid from Gary, Indiana began to work his way into the headlines as well. His name was Michael Jackson.

Those that made their mark during **The Swell Seventies** include:

THE AMERICAN CAST

THE AMERICAN CAST (1971)

KEITH DOLLINS
DAN HALL
PAT McARDLE
SCOTT McDOWELL
JEFF ROY
SCOTT WALLACE

Popular in the 1970s, this Indianapolis band originated at North Central High School. Originally entitled the Screamin' A's, they later became "The American Cast."

AMNESTY Left to right (back): Curt Alexander – James Massie – Calvin Williams – Joe Trotter – Damon Malone – Rafael Barnes – Geno Johnson (front): Herman Walker

Let the Good Times Roll

AMNESTY

CURT ALEXANDER
RAFAEL BARNES
GENO JOHNSON
DAMON MALONE
JAMES MASSIE
JOE TROTTER
HERMAN WALKER
CALVIN WILLIAMS

This Indianapolis R&B soul group was formed in the early 1970s. Recordings include "Lord Help Me/Three Cheers For My Baby" on Two West Records, and "Everybody Who Wants To Be Free," on the Lamp label.

BLACK MAGIC

ALLEN (TURK) BURKE
DUANE "BUZZARD" GARVIN
JOE JACKSON
DOBY LONDON

Formed in 1973, this Indianapolis quartet became a trio after the parting of original drummer Duane Garvin. Black Magic began playing in Indianapolis clubs such as the End Zone and later performed with many national acts. The group featured keyboardist Allen "Turk" Burke, born and raised in Indianapolis. Burke attended Shortridge High School, and began playing professionally when he was around sixteen. He continued to perform with such artists as Patti LaBelle, the Bluebells, and the Spinners. That gig provided the opportunity for him to become music arranger and a permanent band member of The Spinners. In 1974, Allen toured with the famous Marvin Gaye. He later moved back to Indiana to join the local group Fresh. He then formed the group Fingers. He continues to be music arranger and keyboardist for the Spinners.

BLACK MAGIC (1973)
Left to right: Doby London – Allen (Turk) Burke – Joe Jackson

THE CHAMPION BAND

BRUCE "SNOOKY" COONS
BOB JONES
CHARLIE "CHUCK" KENDAL
DAVID "BEAUGIE" WAIT
LOREN "LO" WOODS

This rock group from Indianapolis was formed around 1975. Original members were Jason Becket, David Miller and former Roadmaster musician Adam Smasher (Asher Benruby). Around 1976, Adam Smasher and David Miller left the group and were replaced by the members listed above. In the 1980s, Adam Smasher became a popular DJ, and Loren "Lo" Woods performed with the band Jubal. In 1991, Woods recorded a solo album entitled "It Might Take Years."

DARLENE DOLLAR (DOWLER)
(DARLENE EARLY)

An Indianapolis native, Darlene Dollar began her singing career when she was fourteen. She performed at local teen clubs and record hops in the early 1960s. In the 1970s, she toured the local nightclub circuit. Darlene was the vocalist with her brother's band, Bobby Dark and The Chain Reaction, and later performed with the group, Sunshine Way. After moving to Daytona Beach, Darlene joined the group Tyme. She is active in the music business.

DARLENE DOWLER
with SUNSHINE WAY (1970)

THE CHAIN REACTION (1972)
Left to right (front): Bobby Dark – Darlene Dowler – Gary Thaxton
Left to right (back): Doug Sterns – Paul Gray – John Scott – (unidentified) – Ron Schrock – Gil Work

Let the Good Times Roll

THE FAITH BAND

DAVE BARNES
DAVE BENNETT
JOHN CASCELLA
MARK CAWLEY
CARL STORIE

The Faith Band may be the longest running band to emerge from the Indianapolis area. Formed as the Chosen Few in 1967, they evolved into group Limousine five years later. In 1973, they changed their name to The Faith Band. They recorded "Dancin' Shoes" in 1978. It reached the #54 spot on the Billboard charts. In 1979, they peaked at the #76 position with "You're My Weakness." Both were recorded on the Mercury label. One member, Carl Storie, continues to entertain in the Indianapolis area. In the 1990s, he performed with the Alligator Brothers and later produced and recorded his own CD. Band

THE FAITH BAND (1978)
Left to right: Carl Storie – John Casella (keyboards) – Dave Barnes (drums) – Mark Cawley (bass) – Dave Bennett (guitar)

member John Cascella recorded and toured with the John Mellencamp band. He died of a heart attack on November 14, 1992. The Faith Band recordings include "Faith" (1973), United Artists Records, "Excuse Me…I Just Cut An Album" (1977), Village Records. And "Rock 'n Romance" (1978), "Face To Face" (1979) and "Vital Signs" (1979) all recorded on the Village/Phonogram label.

THE FIFTH ADMENDMENT

LARRY GOSHEN
PAUL GRAY
LOUIE McCANE
TOM RODGERS
JOHN SCOTT

Formed in 1975, this Indianapolis band performed top forty cover tunes on the Indiana nightclub circuit. Saxophonist John Scott later joined the Witness band and bassist Tom Rodgers became an Indianapolis policeman.

THE FIFTH ADMENDMENT (1975)
Left to right (back): John Scott – Tom Rodgers – Paul Gray (front): Louie McCane – Larry Goshen

RICHARD "RICK" FINCH (K.C. AND THE SUNSHINE BAND)

Richard Finch was born January 23, 1954 in Indianapolis. Finch played bass guitar and was an important member of the national recording group, K.C. & The Sunshine Band. He co-wrote some of their biggest hits, including "Shake Your Booty" and "Get Down Tonight." In 1975, it became number one on the Billboard charts. Another Sunshine hit penned by Richard and KC (Harry Wayne Casey) was "That's The Way I Like It." Richard also co-wrote, "Rock Your Baby" for singer George McCrae. In 1974, that song became number one on the Billboard charts in both the United States and the United Kingdom.

FINGERS

ALLEN "TURK" BURKE
BOB SCHUSTER
RUSSELL TAYLOR

Formed in the late 1970s, this popular Indiana group consisted of three talented musicians, Allen "Turk" Burke from Indianapolis, Bob Schuster from Evansville, and Russell Taylor from Anderson. Bob Schuster started his musical career by playing the French horn and studying classical music at Ball State University. Russell Taylor was singing professionally at the age of sixteen. Two years later he became a percussionist. In 1976, he signed with United Artists, and recorded

FINGERS (1979)
Clockwise from top: Russell Taylor – Allen (Turk) Burke – Bob Schuster

one album with the Peddler band entitled, "Street Corner Stuff."The Fingers trio performed in some of the most popular nightclubs in Indianapolis and also toured the United States. They performed locally at clubs such as Pierpont's, the Hilton and the popular Glass Parrot.
(For information on Allen "Turk" Burke, refer to "Fresh" and "Magic" in this section.)

Let the Good Times Roll

FIVE EASY PIECES

CHUCK CUNNINGHAM
CHARLIE HINKLE
BONNIE MC DOWELL
ROBIN MC DOWELL
LES SZIGETHY

Formed in 1972, the Five Easy Pieces performed on the Indiana nightclub circuit. They entertained at such clubs as the Garage in Broad Ripple, and Steckleys in Carmel. This group has opened for such acts as Three Dog Night, The Lettermen and comedian, Rich Little. The Five Easy Pieces continue to perform in the Indianapolis area.

FRESH

ALLEN "TURK" BURKE
BILL LANCTON
DOBY LONDON
RAY PETRONZIO
KATHY STRAKIS

Fresh was formed in Indianapolis in 1974. It was one of the most popular funk and R&B bands to play in the area. The group performed at top Indiana nightclubs such as the Sheraton East, the Enterprise and the Vogue. They toured extensively in over twenty states. Keyboardist Allen "Turk" Burke performed with many major stars such as Marvin Gaye, the Spinners and Patti LaBelle. Bill Lancton performs with the popular Indianapolis band Dog Talk. He has recorded two CD's under his own name, "Lanctones" (1995) and

FIVE EASY PIECES (1973)
Left to right: Chuck Cunningham – Bonnie McDowell – Charlie Hinkle – Robin McDowell – Les Szigethy

FIVE EASY PIECES
(RAM-A-LAM & THE DING DONGS)

FRESH (1976)
Left to right: Doby London – Kathy Strakis – Bill Lancton – Ray Petronzio – Allen (Turk) Burke

Let the Good Times Roll

"Yeah, Man" (1999). Fresh recorded one album in the 1970s, but it was never released. Other members of Fresh were Rob McCoy, Bill Knipe, Don Davidson, Russell Taylor and Bob Schuster. Fresh disbanded in 1978.

JACK GILFOY

Indianapolis-born Jack Gilfoy began playing drums at the age of ten. He studied percussion at Indiana University and then continued studies with jazz drummers Shelly Manne, Joe Morello and Peter Erskine. Gilfoy performed with such artists as Sonny & Cher, Ben E. King, Johnny Mathis, the Marvelettes, and the Spinners. In 1965, Gilfoy opened a recording studio in Bloomington. He recorded Roadmaster, the Wright Brothers Overland Stage, and John Mellencamps first album, "Chestnut Street Incident." For thirty years, Gilfoy was drummer for the Henry Mancini Orchestra. In 1971, he toured for a short time with the king himself, Elvis Presley.

JIM GERRARD and JACK GILFOY
Live on WFBM-TV (1968)

GIZMOS

TIM CARROLL
STEVE FEIKES
PHIL HUNDLEY
DALE LAWRENCE
SHADOW MYERS
TED NIEMIEC
BILLY NIGHTSHADE
ROBBIE WISE

The Indiana-based Gizmos, composed of different members, performed together from 1975 through 1981. Recordings produced in the 1970s were recently re-released on Gulcher, an underground record label originally based in Bloomington. John Mellencamp appeared briefly on one of their recordings, "Boring, Part 1," performing back-up guitar and vocals.

Let the Good Times Roll

GOOD SEED

DOUG ADAMS
GREG ANDERSON
CHRIS BROWNING
RICH GOOTEE
BILLY WARREN

This group from Indiana was formed in the mid-1970s. They recorded two albums, "Rooted & Grounded" (1974), and self-titled "Good Seed" (1976), on Village Records.

JIMMY GUILFORD BAND
(THREE WAY STREET)

ERROLL GRANDY
JIMMY GUILFORD
MINGO JONES
DANNY SMITH

This band performed on the Indianapolis nightclub circuit. Organist Erroll Grandy and bassist Mingo Jones were popular players on the jazz circuit. Jones continues to perform in the Indianapolis area. Grandy died in June of 1991. Guilford is a regular cast member of the American Cabaret Theatre.

JIMMY GUILFORD BAND (1978)
Left to right: Mingo Jones – Jimmy Guilford – Erroll Grandy – Danny Smith

JOHN HIATT

John Hiatt was born in Indianapolis, August 20, 1952. Influenced by black artists such as the Isley Brothers and Otis Redding, he purchased a guitar at a young age and taught himself how to play. Two of the early bands John joined were, "The Four Fifth," and "Joe Lynch and the Hangmen." In the early 1970's, Hiatt moved to Nashville and began his songwriting career for the famous Tree Publishing House. Country singer Tracey Nelson recorded several of his songs. John Hiatt recorded his own songs on his first album entitled, "Hanging 'Round The Observatory" (1974). He released records on Epic, MCA, Geffen, A&M, and Capitol. Hiatt records for the Vanguard label, and his first release "Crossing Muddy Waters," (1999) was nominated for a Grammy Award in the "Best Traditional Blues Album" category.

Let the Good Times Roll

HYJINKS
(EMPIRE)

ALBERT BEARMAN
JOHN DINWIDDIE
DALLAS MILLER
AL ROTH

This Indiana band was formed in the late 1970s. After the replacement of bassist Dallas Miller with Jayson Jones, Hyjinks became Empire. It was successful in the Indianapolis area. A recording was released on the 2nd "Home Grown" album. Later they became the opening band for John "Cougar" Mellencamp at Market Square Arena in Indianapolis.

JERMAINE JACKSON

Jermaine Jackson was born in Gary in 1954. He was an original member of the Jackson Family Singers before joining the Jackson Five singing group in 1964. After a successful tour with the Jacksons, Jermaine recorded his first solo album in 1972. It was titled simply, "Jermaine." His forty-five recording single debut, "That's How Love Goes" climbed to the #46 spot on the Billboard charts. In 1973, he recorded "Daddy's Home," which hit the top 10 earning Jermaine a gold record. He recorded many other albums and singles in the 1980s, providing a fine reputation as a solo artist. He continues to perform for the Jacksons as a soloist. In September of 2001, Jermaine joined his brothers, including Michael, for a 20-year reunion concert at New York's Madison Square Garden.

MICHAEL JACKSON

Michael Jackson was born on August 29, 1958, in Gary. He began performing at age five. In 1964, Michael joined his brothers to form The Jackson Five. In 1971, Michael began his solo career for Motown Records. "Got To Be There" hit the charts, and propelled him to stardom. Michael recorded many songs in the 1970s, but in 1982, under the direction of producer Quincy Jones, "Thriller" was released. It sold over 40 million copies worldwide, and became #1 in the United States and the United Kingdom. The recording received

MICHAEL JACKSON

twelve Grammy nominations. It also produced a run of successful hit singles, each accompanied by a promotional video that widened the scope of the genre. To celebrate his 30-year career, CBS television produced a two-day concert at Madison Square Garden in New York. The event was held September 7 and 10, 2001, and included a performance with Britney Spears and a twenty-year reunion of the Jackson Five.

JUBAL BAND (1975)
Left to right (front): Steve Newbold – Nancy Dorsey – Dave Zerfas (back): Larry McCullough – Bryan Zerfas – Howard Phillips

JUBAL

NANCY DORSEY
LARRY McCULLOUGH
STEVE NEWBOLD
HOWARD PHILLIPS
BRYAN ZERFAS
DAVE ZERFAS

Jubal, a popular band from Indianapolis, was formed in 1975. Later members include Mark Burton, Jeff Gardner, Chick McHenry, Charlie Smith, Pat Smith and John Smith.

KHAZAD DOOM

JACK EADON
STEVE "CROW" HILKIN
TOM SIEVERS
AL YATES

This Gary Indiana band recorded one album in 1970 entitled, "Level 6 ½," on the LPL label. It is listed between $800 to $1200 in the Collectors Price Guide.

THE LATE SHOW

RICK CLAYTON
DON MAIN
MARK MORAN
CHRIS PYLE

This group from Indianapolis was formed in the late 1970s. They recorded one album in 1980 entitled, "Portable Pop." It was recorded on the Rave label.

Let the Good Times Roll

The group appeared around the Midwest and opened for many top name acts including The Pretenders, Dr. Hook and Huey Lewis and the News. In the 1980s, they changed their name to Recordio.

BRAD LONG

Logansport-native Brad Long was born in 1954. He began his music career in 1967 as a percussionist. Long then studied the guitar and later became successful on the bass and keyboards. He began playing with the group Celebrate in 1971, and in 1973 joined the band Tobias. He later performed as a single act. In 1978, he recorded "Love Me Again/Come To Me" on the Music Stand label. In 1981, Long recorded for the compilation album, "Battle of the Garages." Brad Long continues to perform special concerts in the Logansport area.

BRAD LONG (1978)

MADISON ZANE

PAULA BARGE'
JIM BENGE
STEVE DRYBREAD
DON EWIGLEBEN
LARRY SAUER
JOE STOUT

This lounge band from Indianapolis was formed in 1976. They recorded one single.

MADISON ZANE (1976)
Left to right (back): Steve Drybread – Jim Benge – Larry Sauer – Joe Stout
(front): Don Ewigleben – Paula Barge'

Let the Good Times Roll

MANCHILD

MANCHILD (1977)

CHUCK BUSH
KENNY EDMONDS
REGGIE GRIFFIN
ROBERT PARSON
DARYL SIMMONS

The band Manchild, was formed in Indianapolis. They recorded for the Chi-Sound label around 1977. Later, singer Kenny Edmonds joined his brothers Kevon and Melvin in their group, After 7. Kenny later became known as Babyface, producing artists such as Toni Braxton, Boyz II Men, and Madonna. (Above photo – Kenny Edmonds, back row, third from left.)

DONALD McPHERSON

Indianapolis-born Donald McPherson was an important member of the popular group, The Main Ingredient. They were very successful in 1970 with their hit recording of "I'm So Proud" for RCA Records. The Main Ingredient was originally called, "The Poets." They had recorded "Merry Christmas Baby" on the Red Bird Label in 1965. In 1971, Donald McPherson died of leukemia. His replacement in The Main Ingredient was none other than singer Cuba Gooding, father of Academy Award nominated actor, Cuba Gooding Jr.

JOHN (COUGAR) MELLENCAMP

John Mellencamp was born on October 7, 1951 in Seymour. He began his musical career by entertaining in high school. Mellencamp played with the band, "Crepe Soul" for 18 months before

JOHN MELLENCAMP

Let the Good Times Roll

being kicked out for his inability to sing. He joined "Snakepit Banana Barn" and after graduating from high school, formed the group "Trash." It included guitarist Larry Crane. Mellencamp later enjoyed great success by recording under the name of John Cougar. Two popular hits were, "Hurts So Good" and "Jack And Diane." In 1983, Mellencamp released his first album under the name of John Mellencamp, and his recordings continued to climb the charts. Mellencamp recorded eleven albums from 1976 through 1989 for the Riva label and then Mercury and MCA. In 1992 he starred in and performed the soundtrack for the movie "Falling From Grace." Various Indiana members of past recording sessions include Kenny Aronoff, John Cascella, Dane Clark, Larry Crane, Liza Germano, Dave Grissom, Toby Myers and Mike Wanchic. Mellencamp released his latest album "Cuttin' Heads," in 2001.

MELTING POT

DICK GENTILE
PAUL HMUROVICH
HOWIE McGURTY
STEVE NICHOLS
JOE RUDD
MICKEY SMITH
JERRY THOMPSON
KENNY TIBBETS
BILL WITHERSPOON

Consisting of musicians from Indianapolis and other surrounding states, the Melting Pot was a great soul group. The group, popular from 1970, was heavy with brass. They recorded one album "Fire Burn, Cauldron Bubble" (1971), on the Ampex label.

OMEGA

JIM HAGANMAN
AL ROTH
MONTE STULTZ
BRUCE WEINGARDT

Four Southport High School students in Indianapolis formed Omega in 1972. This group played locally at the Sherwood and other teen clubs.

RAPTURE

RODNEY BORHIC
HARRY EATON
TONY HAYES
PHELDON J. MAJORS
GREG RUSSELL
RODNEY STEPP
HERMAN WALKER
LONNIE WILLIAMS

R&B soul group Rapture was formed in the late 1970s in Indianapolis. The popular group toured the United States and opened for many name acts. Member Rodney Stepp became one of the music directors of the Spinners.

RAPTURE
Left to right: Herman Walker – Rodney Stepp – Greg Russell – Pheldon J. Majors – Harry Eaton – Lonnie Williams – Tony Hayes – Rodney Borhie

RICH KIDS

DEAN CHILDRESS
JIM GARDNER
JEFF HOLT
DAVE WASHBURN
CORKY
WHITEMAN

This Fowler, Indiana group recorded three singles, "Dance Your Way Into My Heart/Always On The Run" (1977), "Oh The Girls/ Young Kingdom" and "You Always Hurt The One You Love/Mars Needs Women," both in 1979.

RICH KIDS (1976)
Left to right: Jim Gardner – Dave Washburn – Dean Childress – Corky Whiteman – Jeff Holt
(Photograph by Rick Childress)

ROADMASTER

RICK BENICK
BOBBY JOHNS
STEPHEN McNALLY
TOBY MYERS
MICHAEL REED
STEPHEN RILEY
ADAM SMASHER

This Indianapolis-based band was discovered at a local nightclub in 1975 by recording artist Todd Rundgren. Roadmaster traveled nationally, and opened for artists such as Ted Nugent, Blue Oyster Cult and Rush. Their first album "Roadmaster"(1976) was recorded for the "Village" label. Later they were signed by "Mercury," and recorded "Sweet Music" (1978), "Hey World" (1979) and "Fortress" (1980). Adam Smasher, one of the original members who recorded only on the first album, later became a popular Indianapolis disc jockey. Bass player Toby Myers joined John Mellencamp's band, and can be heard on some of his early recordings.

ROADMASTER

DAVID LEE ROTH

Born October 10, 1955, in Bloomington, David Lee Roth performed with the Redball Jet band before he was hired to join the popular group, Van Halen. Roth's good looks and flamboyant antics and guitarist Eddie Van Halen's talent made Van Halen one of the most popular bands in the 1970s and 80s. This fame occurred after the band played the bar circuit around Pasadena/Santa Barbara for three years. They first became successful with their self-titled album in 1978. It hit number nineteen on the charts and eventually sold over six million copies. After many successful recordings, Roth became a solo artist in 1985 and released a four-song EP, "Crazy from the Heat." It spun off two hit singles, "California Girls," and the Louis Prima song, "Just a Gigolo/Ain't Got Nobody."

SCREAMIN' GYPSY BANDITS

BRUCE ANDERSON
MARK BINGHAM
TINA LANE
BOB LUCAS
DALE SOPHIEA

This Bloomington-band recorded two LP's, "In The Eye" (1973) and "Dancer Inside You" (1974), both on the BRBQ label. Two members of this band, Bruce Anderson and Dale Sophiea formed the popular San Francisco group, MX 80.

SHILOH MORNING

MARK BOUSE
MARK HANCOCK
JOHN McDOWELL
JEANNIE McGILL
KEN SCHEIDLER

Formed in the mid-1970s, this band played the Indianapolis nightclub circuit. They recorded one album, self-titled "Shiloh Morning" (1974).

THEM CHANGES

THEM CHANGES (1978)
Left to right: Ben Hickman – Larry Goshen – Paul Gray – Bill Dickie

BILL DICKIE
PAUL GRAY
BEN HICKMAN
LARRY GOSHEN

This band was formed in 1978. It played the Indianapolis nightclub circuit when disco was at its peak.

TIMMY THOMAS

Timmy Thomas was born in Evansville on November 13, 1944. An accomplished singer, songwriter and keyboardist, Thomas performed with jazz icons such as Donald Byrd and Cannonball Adderley. After

Let the Good Times Roll

performing session work with the Memphis-based Goldwax label, he embarked on a solo career. In 1972, Timmy Thomas' Polydor recording of "Why Can't We Live Together" hit #3 on the Billboard charts.   He later continued a run of minor R&B hits recorded on Glades Records.

TOBIAS

PAT HAGENE
STEVE KINDER
BRAD LONG
TED PITMAN

Formed in 1973, this band was from the Logansport area. They performed at teen dances and high school events around the northern area of Indiana.

DUKE TUMATOE AND THE ALL-STAR FROGS
DUKE TUMATOE AND THE POWER TRIO

GARY BREWER
L.V. HAMMOND
JAMES HILL
DOCTOR SEUSS
ROBIN STEELE
DUKE TUMATOE

Duke Tumatoe and The All-Star Frogs was formed in the 1970s and performed

DUKE TUMATOE & THE ALL STAR FROGS (1975)
Left to right: Doctor Susses – Gary Brewer – L.V. Hammond – Duke Tumatoe – James Hill

well into the late 1980s. Duke recorded several albums, "Naughty Child" (1981), "Duke Tumatoe And The All Star Frogs" (1982), and "Dukes Up" (1984) on the Blind Pig label. Under the Power Trio name, they recorded "I Like My Job" (1988) on Warner. Duke Tumatoe continues to perform and record around the Indianapolis area. He is a regular guest on the popular Bob & Tom radio program.

DENIECE WILLIAMS

Soul singer Deniece Williams was born Deniece Chandler, June 3, 1951 in Gary. She recorded her first single in the late 1960s for the Chicago based label, Toddlin' Town Records. Williams was hired by Stevie Wonder to join his vocal back-up group, and contributed to four of his albums. After leaving Wonder for a solo career, she recorded her first album, "This Is Niecy" (1976) on Columbia. Williams recorded "Songbird" (1977) and then teamed with Johnny Mathis for the big hits, "Too Much Too Little Too Late" and "That's What Friends Are For"(1978). Williams recorded many songs, but became well known for "Let's Hear It For The Boy" (Columbia 1984) from the soundtrack of "Footloose." A very successful songwriter, she has penned tunes for such artists as Frankie Valli, the Whispers, Stanley Turrentine, Nancy Wilson and many others. In the late 1980s, Williams recorded several gospel albums on the Sparrow label, and "This Is My Song" (1998) on Harmony. Her later recordings were not as successful, but she still remains popular with the R&B audience.

BILL WILSON

Bill Wilson was a singer-songwriter from the Indianapolis area. He recorded several albums, including "Ever Changing Minstrel" (1973) on the Columbia label, "Talking To Stars" (1976) Bar-Bq Records and "Made In The USA" (1980).

THE WRIGHT BROS. OVERLAND STAGE CO.

JOHN MCDOWELL III
RON PERRY
REX THOMAS
STEVE WALKER
TIM WRIGHT
TOM WRIGHT
(Additional members)
JACK GILFOY
KARL HINKLE

Let the Good Times Roll

THE WRIGHT BROTHERS (1980)
Left to right: Tom Wright – Karl Hinkle – Tim Wright

THE WRIGHT BROTHERS

KARL HINKLE
TIM WRIGHT
TOM WRIGHT

Tim and Tom Wright were born in French Lick, Indiana. They first formed the Overland Stage band around 1971, and recorded on their own label, "Wright & Perry Records." Around 1980, Karl Hinkle joined the brothers and they became The Wright Brothers band. They recorded for Warner Bros. Records and then the Mercury label. The Wright Brothers perform a variety of music, Rock & Roll, Country, Bluegrass and Gospel. They have appeared on the Grand Ole Opry, and made special appearances with such entertainers as Bob Hope, Dolly Parton, Ronnie Milsap, and the Coasters, to name a few. The Wright Brothers appeared on several television shows such as "Hee Haw," the "Ralph Emery Show," and the "Today Show." They performed on the soundtrack and appeared in the MGM movie, "Overboard," staring Goldie Hawn and Kurt Russell. Current band members Tom and Tim Wright, John McDowell, and Greg Anderson are still very active in the music business.

Left to right: Tom Wright – Ronnie Milsap – Karl Hinkle – Tim Wright

ZERFAS (1973)
Left to right: Bryan Zerfas – Billy Rice – Mark Tribby – Dave Zerfas – Steve Newbold

ZERFAS

STEVE NEWBOLD
BILLY RICE
MARK TRIBBY
BRYAN ZERFAS
DAVE ZERFAS

Formed in 1973, this Indianapolis band began as the group Zerfas. They later became part of the group Jubal. A rare recording produced in 1973 (a small quantity was pressed) has become a popular collector's item. This album was recorded on the 700

Let the Good Times Roll

West label. Other prerecorded 1970s recordings recently re-surfaced included musicians Paul McBee and the Wright Brother's vocalist Karl Hinkle. Collectors continue to search for them.

1970 NOTABLES

ALLISON TURNER
CALVIN TURNER
CHARLES COTTON
HARRISON TURNER
JAMES DIXON
MELVIN TURNER
MICHAEL BOARDS
PAUL TURNER
RUDY ROSS
TED PATTERSON
TOBY MYERS

Let the Good Times Roll

The Emphatic Eighties

Let the Good Times Roll

The Emphatic Eighties

Ronald Reagan's election as the 40th President of the United States over Jimmy Carter eased the country into the 1980s. George Bush was Vice President and former Nixon loyalist General Alexander Haig became Secretary of State when George Schultz resigned.

Relations between Israel and the U.S. were rocked when spy Jonathan Jay Pollard was exposed while passing secret security documents to America's ally. A Federal judge, unmoved by Pollard's passion to save Israel from doom, imposed a life sentence. Rallies were conducted across the country protesting Pollard's treatment.

President Reagan called the Soviet Union "The Evil Empire," and supported Central American rebels fighting for freedom. A scandal occurred when the president and other members of his administration were criticized for their part in what became known as "The Iran/Contra Affair." Regardless, Reagan trounced Walter Mondale to earn a second term in office in 1984.

A year later, terrorism reared its ugly head when the Italian oceanliner, "The Achille Lauro" was seized. Four hundred and fifty passengers were held hostage including an American who was executed. In 1988, George Bush and Indiana-born Dan Quayle ascended to the White House by defeating Michael Dukakis and Lloyd Bentsen.

Cultural news was headlined when *Ordinary People* won the Academy Award for Best Picture in 1980. Robert De Niro won best actor for Raging Bull, and Sissy Spacek best actress for her role in *Coal Miner's Daughter*. That film was based on the life story of country singer Loretta Lynn. Other films of note during the 80s included *An American Werewolf in London, An Officer and A Gentleman, Raiders of the Lost Ark, Amadeus,* and *Dirty Dancing. Hill Street Blues* became the number one television program.

Popular songs during the 1980s included, "Bettie Davis Eyes," "Abracadabra," "Jack & Diane," and "Flashdance." Indiana-born Michael Jackson contributed such hits as "Bad," Thriller," and "Beat It.

In 1981, the music industry lost three icons when Bill Haley, Harry Chapin, and Hoosier Hoagy Carmichael, composer of "Stardust," died. Celebrities such as John Belushi, Count Basie, and Muddy Waters also died during the decade.

During the 1980s, music flourished in Indiana. Michael Jackson's fame ignited interest in other Hoosier musicians. The styles varied, but famed groups such as Motley Crue and Guns N' Roses featured Indiana talent. Folk singer Carrie Newcomer gained attention, as did the three Mitchell Sisters performing as the Starlettes. John Mellencamp continued to perform hit music, and Henry Lee Summer was popular, as was the jazz-rock group The Mathematicians, the Dancing Cigarettes, and Dow Jones and the Industrials.

Top nightspots in Indiana during the '80s included the Vogue, Bentley's, The Razz ma Tazz, the Enterprise, the Sundance, and the Patio. These clubs provided the springboard for Indiana artists with an eye on the national spotlight. Those that performed during **The Emphatic Eighties** include:

ACID GREEN (1988)
Left to right: Gym Stoffer – Gregg Stewart – John Zeps – Sander Leech – Bob Cripe

ACID GREEN

BOB CRIPE
SANDER LEECH
GREGG STEWART
GYM STOFFER
JOHN ZEPS

This heavy metal band was formed in Indianapolis in 1987 and continued to perform into the mid-1990s. They recorded one EP entitled, "As The World Turns" (1991), on Rusty Low Records, and a CD "Nuciei" (1994), on Augmented Mammaet Records.

AFTER 7

KEVON EDMONDS
MELVIN EDMONDS
KEITH MITCHELL

Formed in 1989 by Indiana University students, After 7 became one of Indiana's most successful R&B/Soul acts. They recorded their first album self-titled, "After 7" (1989), on the Virgin Label. That recording produced four top 10 US singles, and won a Grammy nomination for Best Soul Group. Their second recording, "Taking My Time" (1992), was also recorded on the Virgin Label. Although not listed as one of the members, brother Kenny "Babyface" Edmonds contributed to the first recording. Edmonds returned in 1995 to write three songs, and sing "Honey, Oh How I Need You," for the group's third album, "Reflections."

BIG TWIST AND THE MELLOW FELLOWS

BIG TWIST (LARRY NOLAN)
TERRY OGOLINI
PETE SPECIAL

Born in Terre Haute in 1938, Larry Nolan performed under the name, Big Twist. He was drummer and vocalist for the 1950s band, Mellow Fellows. In the 1970s, this group performed behind artists such as James Brown and Big Joe Turner, and recorded on the Flying Fish and Alligator Record labels. In the 1980s, Nolan recorded several albums under the Big Twist name,

Let the Good Times Roll

including "Big Twist And The Mellow Fellows" and "Big Twist Playing For Keeps" (1983) on Alligator Records. "One Track Mind" on Red Lightnin,' and "Live From Chicago" (1987), returning to the Alligator label. Larry Nolan died of a heart attack March 14, 1990 in Broadview, Illinois.

BLUE PRINT

JOHNNY ATKINS
MARK BULLOCK
MIKE KOPACEK
MARK STEINHARDT
KENNY NEAL
BOBBY TOON

COUSINS FROM VENUS

JENNIFER AYERS
TIM AYERS
SARGE GLANTON
MARK KENNEDY
PEABODY

Other members include: SREYA CHAMBERS, CZM and JOHNNY VULCAN

THE DANCING CIGARETTES

EMILY BONUS
MICHAEL GITLIN
TIMOTHY NOE
JACLYN ODDI
JOHN TERRILL
G. DON TRUBOY

This Bloomington-based band was formed in 1980. They recorded one EP entitled, "Dancing Cigarettes" (1981) on the Gulcher label.

DELIVERANCE (1987)
Left to right (back roll): James Fountain – Kevin Resnover
– Kenny Phelps – Mark Plummer – Emmanuel Officer (front): Bill
Ellis – Keith Phelps

DELIVERANCE

BILL ELLIS
JAMES FOUNTAIN
EMMANUEL OFFICER
KEITH PHELPS
KENNY PHELPS
MARK PLUMMER
KEVIN RESNOVER

Formed in 1987, this Indianapolis Gospel/Soul group recorded many gospel songs. Singer Emmanuel Officer later became a member of the Kenny (Baby Face) Edmonds group, Manchild. Drummer Kenny Phelps and his Brother Keith recorded backup for such groups as El Debarge.

DOW JONES AND THE INDUSTRIALS

DAVE BEHNKE
CHRIS CLARK
BRAD GARTON
GREG HORN
TIM NORTH
JENNY SWEANY

This was a West Lafayette-based group that recorded one self-titled EP on the Gulch label (1980).

DARREN DOWLER

Indianapolis-born Darren Dowler grew up in a musical family. Darren's father, Danny Dollar (Dowler) began performing in the late 1950s. His mother Darlene, who also performed in the late 1950s, fronted her own band and entertained at some of the top nightspots in Florida. After moving to Daytona Beach, Darren

DARREN DOWLER

Let the Good Times Roll

THE LETTERMEN
Left to right: Donovan Scott Tea – Darren Dowler – Tony Butala

THE TYME (1988)
Left to right: Darlene (Dowler) Grigsby – Darren Dowler – Brian – Lea – Ken – Rob

started his musical career by singing at the age of fourteen. At the age of eighteen, he moved to Westport, Connecticut where he formed his own group, the Darren Dowler Band. Darren also entered the acting field and performed in the musical, "Grease." He later landed small rolls in such television shows as *The Swamp Thing, The Adventures of Superboy* and *As The World Turns*. In the 1980s, Darren performed with his mother's band Tyme, and in the 1990s joined the national singing group, The Lettermen. He continues to tour with The Lettermen and performs in concerts across the country.

THE EQUALIZERS

GLEN CORNICK
JINX DAWSON
MICHAEL MONARCH
LINDA NARDINI
STEVE ROSS

Indianapolis natives, and ex-Coven members Jinx Dawson and Steve Ross formed this Los Angles band in the mid-1980s. The group also featured bass player Glen Cornick, a former member of Jethro Tull, and Michael Monarch, guitarist from the Steppenwolf band.

THE EQUALIZERS (1985)
Left to right: Glenn Cornick –Jinx Dawson – Michael Monarch

THE FIRST IMPRESSION

WENDY AUSCHERMAN
STEVE MATHEWS
KEVIN MC DONALD
JEFF REED

This band from the Indianapolis area was formed in 1985. They performed at local nightspots and special events. Their unique form of jazz and dance music earned them popularity. They still perform, but not with the original members.

THE FIRST IMPRESSION (1986)
Left to right: Jeff Reed – Wendy Auscherman – Kevin McDonald – Steve Mathews

THE GIRLS

BEAU BRIAKLEY
JULIE GERARD
BEA ISAACS
PAM LEE
KELLY OLIVER

The Girls were originally formed in 1985 by bassist Bea Isaacs, guitarist Julie Gerard, and drummer Kelly Oliver. Pam Lee joined them in 1986 and Beau

Let the Good Times Roll

Briakley became a member in 1987. The popular all-girl band toured the United States and Canada, and once a year, from 1987 through 1992, was booked into one of the top nightclubs in Las Vegas. In 1999, The Girls changed their name to Drama Queen, and recorded their first CD. Drama Queen performs in the Indianapolis area.

GROUP THEROPY

ALBERT BEARMAN
JOHN DINWIDDIE
MIKE PIPES
JIMMY WILLIAMS

Composing the original line-up of Group Theropy were Albert Bearman, Danny Daubkins, Mark Iverson, Kim Madget and Bruce Wiengart. The members in the photograph played together in 1988. This unit stayed together for two years, but Group Theropy, with different members, lasted into the 1990s. Starting out as an R&B Motown style band, the group later worked into the top 40 rock n' roll market.

GROUP THEROPY
Left to right: Jimmy Williams – Albert Bearman – John Dinwiddle – Mike Pipes.
Photo by Jimmy Mack

GUNS N' ROSES

This heavy-metal band was formed in Los Angeles by two Indiana musicians, Axl Rose (William Bailey) and Izzy Stridlin (Jeff Isbell). Both were born in Lafayette, Indiana. In 1986, Guns n' Roses recorded "Appetite For Destruction" on the Geffen label. It reached number one on the Billboard charts for five weeks and was a staple on the charts for nearly three years. The band continued to be popular in the 1980s & '90s despite controversy among the performers and with the media. Axl Rose and new members of Guns n' Roses performed at the Hard Rock Café in Las Vegas on New Years Eve, 2001.

BARBARA HIGBIE

Michigan-born Barbara Higbie was raised in Speedway, Indiana. After studying classical piano at the age of thirteen, she moved with her

BARBARA HIGBIE (1982)
Photo by Irene Young

Let the Good Times Roll

family to Ghana, West Africa. Barbara began her professional music career in the early 1980s in the San Francisco Bay area. She performed with artists such as Darol Anger, Mike Marshall, Todd Phillips, David Balakrishnan and Rob Wasserman. In 1982, Barbara recorded "Tideline" on the Windham Hill label with violinist Darol Anger. She recorded an album with Teresa Trull entitled "Unexpected" (1983). The *Boston Globe* named it as one of the ten best albums of the year. In 1985, Barbara recorded at the Montreux Jazz Festival in Switzerland with violinist Darol Anger. The recording on the Windham Hill label included Mike Marshall, Todd Phillips and Andy Narell. The group successfully recorded three albums under the Montreux name. Barbara earned a Grammy nomination for one of her own compositions. She has performed and recorded on over 40 albums, and in 1990 recorded a solo album on the Windham Hill label, "Signs of Life." It was named one of the ten best albums of the year by the *Washington Post*. Other recordings of note are "Barbara Higbie—I Surrender" (1996), and "Playtime" (1997) with Barbara Higbie and Teresa Trull, both on Slow Baby Records.

HUGO SMOOTH BAND

RON BRINSON
JOAN E. HALL
WAYNE HALL
BRIAN E. PAULSON

This Indiana group from 1980 recorded one album self-titled "Hugo Smooth Band," on the Big Time Record label.

ILLICIT AFFAIR (1983)
Left to right (top): Brad Estes – Jeff Holt – Jim Gardner
(bottom): Ron Coffman – Dean Childress. Photograph by Rick
Childress

ILLICIT AFFAIR

DEAN CHILDRESS
RON COFFMAN
JAY DAVIS
BRAD ESTES
JIM GARDNER
JEFF HOLT

This band from the Fowler, Indiana area was formed in 1983. They recorded two 45's, "Girls In The USA/Leather Jacket On" (1984) and "History Is Made At Night/You Move Me" (1985).

Let the Good Times Roll

JANET JACKSON

Let the Good Times Roll

JANET JACKSON

Janet was born on May 16, 1966, in Gary. She began performing at the age of seven with her famous brothers, The Jackson Five. At age ten, Jackson played the television character Penny Gordon on the popular show "Good Times." In 1982, Janet recorded her first hit "Young Love" on the A&M Label. Later in the 1980s & 90s, Janet was popular with her top R&B hit recordings "Control" (1986), "Rhythm Nation 1814" (1989) and "Janet (1993). She acted in the film, Poetic Justice, in 1983. Janet continues to perform on tour, and in 2001, released the CD "All For You," on the Virgin label.

LA TOYA JACKSON

LA TOYA JACKSON

Born in Gary in 1956, La Toya Jackson was the fifth oldest child in the Jackson family. Her professional music career started around 1975 when she joined the Jackson's after they left Motown and regrouped. She recorded three albums in the 1980s, "La Toya Jackson," "My Special Love" on Polydor Records, and "Heart Don't Lie" for the Private Label. One of La Toya's original songs, "Raggae Nights" was recorded by Jimmy Cliff and became a huge success in France.

JUBAL BAND

JOHN DINWIDDIE
STEVE NEWBOLD
HOWARD PHILLIPS
BRYAN ZERFAS
DAVE ZERFAS

This group is a later version of Jubal that was formed in 1981. The band had originated in the 1970s.

JUBAL BAND (1981)
Left to right: Steve Newbold – Dave Zerfas – Howard Phillips – Bryan Zerfas – John Dinwiddie

KILO

CHARLES
JOHN ENGELLAND
GEORGIA
SHAWN PELTON
DAVE RANDLE
JEFFREY STUART
CRYSTAL TALIEFERO

Formed in the mid-1980s, this funk-rock band was based in Bloomington.
Some members were students of Indiana University and were involved
in the *Soul Review*, a student jazz music organization. Member Crystal
Taliefero later joined the John Mellencamp band, and then toured with Bob
Seger.

THE LAST FOUR (4) DIGITS

S. V. GRIDGESBY
J. HUFFAKER
J. KOSS
MR. SCIENCE
M. SHEETS
R. WORTH
XAX

This Indianapolis group was formed in 1981. They recorded one EP entitled "Big Picture" on the Hardly Record label.

LATEX NOVELTIES

RANDY CREEP
OTIS JAYNE MANSFIELD
NOX
PETER PILLS
ANDY REYIA

The repertoire of this 1985 avant-garde band from the Indianapolis area consisted of original material. Their strange fashion of dress and strange titles of songs created a wide following.

LIGHT (1984)

Let the Good Times Roll

LIGHT

JEFF HORNBECK
JEFF LANCE
JOHN W. McDOWELL III
STEVE WALKER

An Indianapolis band from the 1980s.

MALACHI

JOHN DINWIDDIE
KEVIN "FLASH" FERRELL
HERALD GOOCH
CHARLEY GRAHN
RICKY KNOX
ROBYN STEEL
DANNY WILLIAMS

Indianapolis-based Malachi was originally formed in the early 1970s. The group in the photograph comprised the 1985 version. Malachi played the Indiana area, performing proms, private functions and appearing occasionally at the popular Vogue nightclub.

MALACHI
Left to right (top): Danny Williams – Robyn Steel – Herald Gooch – Ricky Knox (front): John Dinwiddie – Kevin (Flash) Ferrell – Charley Grahn

MACUMBA DENTISTS

KEVIN KAISER
BILL LEVIN
JOHNNY QUEST
ROBIN REUTER
CAPTAIN STEELE

This Indianapolis-based band was formed in the 1980s.

MICK MARS
(Bob Deal)

Mick Mars, a/k/a Bob Deal, was born April 3, 1956 in Terre Haute. In the early 1980s, Mick placed a classified advertisement in the Los Angeles Times that read "Loud Rude Aggressive Guitarist Available." Contacted, he began to play guitar and vocalize with the newly formed band, Motley Crue. The band included Tommy Lee (Bass) on drums. The heavy metal band climbed to the charts with "Shout at the Devil" (1983), "Theatre of Pain"

MOTLEY CRUE
Third from left: Mick Mars (Bob Deal)

(1985) and "Girls, Girls, Girls" (1987). Mick Mars continues to perform with Motley Crue. They released a reunion album "Generation Swine" (1997) that climbed to the #5 position on the pop charts.

MATHEMATICIANS

BOB FIELDS
EDDY HUMPHREY
KEVIN KOUTS
LARRY McCULLOUGH

This jazz-fusion rock group from the Indianapolis area was formed in 1989. Their recording of "Factor Of Four" (1996) included guest artists Cathy Morris on violin and Yun Hui on keyboards.

MATHEMATICIANS (1989)
Left to right: Kevin Kouts – Bob Fields – Larry McCullough – Eddy Humphrey

CARRIE NEWCOMER

CARRIE NEWCOMER

Carrie Newcomer was born in Elkhart, Indiana. She wrote her first song after graduating from high school. During college while studying visual arts, she paid her dues by performing in bars and bowling alleys. After college, she taught music during the day and spent her evenings doing what she loved best, performing. In the mid-1980s, Carrie performed with a band from Lafayette entitled Stone Soup. She recorded two albums with that group before leaving in 1989 to pursue her own career. Carrie recorded her first solo album on the Windchime label in 1991 entitled "Visions and Dreams." She currently records for Rounder Records. Carrie has opened nationally for artists such as Alison Krauss & Union Station, and has performed at Carnegie Hall and the London Royal Festival Theater. Carrie Newcomer is an extraordinary writer who pens her songs from personal experiences, and the experience of others.

JOHN O'BANION

Kokomo native John O'Banion recorded two albums: A self titled release in 1981 and "Danger" (1982), both on the Elektra label. His release of a single in 1981 entitled "I Love You Like I Never Loved Before" climbed into the top 100 on the Billboard charts.

THE PANICS

ERIC WHITE
JOHN BARGE
MIKE OST
JOHNNY CARSON

This Bloomington-based band recorded one EP, "The Panics" (1980) on the Gulcher (201) label.

THE PASSION

"RILEY" GARY ANDERSON
BRUCE COOMBS
MIKE HALL
BUTCH SANDLIN
JOE SCHREINER

The Passion was formed in Indianapolis in the mid-1980s. It included members of two past bands, Joe Schreiner, former keyboard player from Playmate, and Butch Sandlin, former drummer of Bodacious. The rest is all Passion.

PORT RASIN BAND

JEFF MARTIN
JIM TE RONDE
BRIAN WOOLDRIDGE
SCOTT WOOLDRIDGE

This band was formed in the early 1980s in Kokomo. Two members, Brian and Scott Wooldridge composed the soundtrack for the television series, *Party of Five.*

P.S. DUMP YOUR BOYFRIEND

KEVIN BAXTER
DAVE HOLCOMB
RICK LONG
OLIVER MORRIS
PHIL PIERLE

RASTABILLY REBELS

RANDY CREEP
MARK CUTSINGER
CAPTAIN STEELE
BRUCE STUCKEY
THOM WOODARD

RECORDIO

RICK CLAYTON
DON MAIN
MARK MORAN
CHRIS PYLE

PS DUMP YOUR BOYFRIEND (1985)

Recordio was formed in Indianapolis around the mid-1980s. Formally entitled the Late Show, this group played original material, top 40, and classic R&B.

RED BEANS AND RICE (1989)
Left to right (top): Tom Becklehimer – Yun Hui –
(Bottom): Billy Young – Ed Jarman

Let the Good Times Roll

RED BEANS AND RICE

TOM BECKLEHIMER
ED JARMAN
BILLY YOUNG
YUN HUI

Red Beans & Rice was formed 1989 in Indianapolis. Fronted by vocalist and keyboardist Yun Hui, the band played a progressive style of rhythm & blues. Yun Hui (pronounced Uni) is a native of South Korea and moved to the United States at the age of seven. After studying classical voice and piano at Indiana University, Yun Hui traveled for three years around the United States before returning to Indiana. Red Beans and Rice recordings include "Staples" (1993), "Eat Big" (1996), "Yes We Can" (1999) and "Live Hot Beans" (2001). Red Beans & Rice disbanded in 2001, and Yun Hui relocated in Hollywood, California. Other members of this group were Robert Coleman Jr., Darren Stroud and Jeff Triwedi.

RODS AND CONES

P.K. LAVENGOOD
RUSS LEVITT
DAVE POST MERRIS

Originator P.K. Lavengood performed with several local bar bands in the early 1980s, including the band Safari. He later played with the Joe Ely Band, Storyville and John Mellencamp. Rods and Cones was formed in Bloomington in 1984. They opened for many name artists, including Stevie Ray Vaughn. They recorded an EP in the 1980s, and produced a video entitled "Boys Will be Boys." It received airplay on MTV.

JOHN "BJ" ROGERS

Originally from Oregon, Rogers spent most of his later years in Indianapolis. A self-taught guitarist, Rogers was quite successful performing rock-a-billy and rock n' roll oldies. He traveled the country as a performing artist. In 1985,

JOHN "BJ" ROGERS (1985)

he appeared at the Buddy Holly Convention in Texas. His recording of "Buddy Holly Days/49 Lincoln" (1985) on Fraternity Records is rapidly becoming a collector's item. Other recordings include a CD "Tech-No-Colour" (1995), on Rivertown Records.

R.S.V.P.
Left to right: Danny Brown – Kent Weineke – Scott Bailey
– Brian Christopher

R.S.V.P.

SCOTT BAILEY
DANNY BROWN
BRIAN CHRISTOPHER
KENT WEINEKE

This Indianapolis band performed on the local nightclub circuit in the 1980s. One of the members, Scott Bailey is the son of Delbert Bailey, a popular singer from the 1960s and 70s.

SALLY'S DREAM

JENNY DAVIS
CHRIS DICKINSON
CYN HAMMOND
EMILY JACKSON

In 1985, this Bloomington-based rock band received rave reviews while performing on the local nightclub scene. Opening for national acts, they worked in such clubs as the Second Story and Jake's.

THE STARLETTES (THE FABULOUS STARLETTES)

JULIE MITCHELL
MARY MITCHELL
ZANNA MITCHELL

This popular 1980s sister trio was in great demand around the Indianapolis area. Their showmanship and perfection for singing made the Starlettes stand out as performers. Zanna later became a member of the popular Alligator Brothers band. She continues to perform in the Indianapolis area with the group Zanna Doo.

Let the Good Times Roll

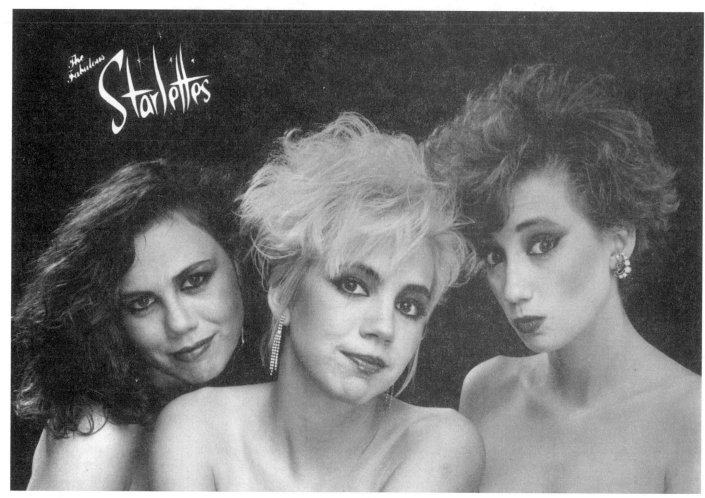

THE STARLETTES (1985)
Left to right: Julie Mitchell – Mary Mitchell – Zanna Mitchell

CARL STORIE

Carl Storie was born in Muncie and attended Ball State University. In the mid-1960s, while attending high school, Carl watched the Beatles at the Indianapolis Coliseum. Inspired by the performance, Carl and his friends sold their prized possessions to purchase musical instruments. He then formed the group Chosen Few. After recording a few singles on the Denim and Talum labels, the group was signed by RCA. Carl performed with such groups as Limousine, The Faith Band and the Alligator Brothers, and in 1999 released his own CD. He continues to entertain in the Indianapolis area with his own group, The Carl Storie Band.

Left to right: Mark Collie – John Casella – Bill Brunt – Carl Storie

CARL STORIE

Let the Good Times Roll

HENRY LEE SUMMER

Popular singer and musician Henry Lee Summer was born on July 5, 1955 in Brazil, Indiana. A self-taught musician on the drums, piano and guitar, he became a top entertainer. Summer performed in many of the top nightclubs throughout the midwest. In 1982 he released his first single "Sweet Love." In 1984, he recorded his first LP "Stay With Me," and in 1985 released "Time For Big Fun." In 1988, Henry signed for CBS Associated Records, and released the self-titled "Henry Lee Summer." That same year he appeared on MTV in his own music video. Other albums released by Summer were "I've Got Everything" (1989), "Way Past Midnight" (1991), "Slam Dunk" (1993), "Smoke And Mirrors" (1999), "Live" (2000) and "Big Drum" (2001). Some of the musicians who performed in the Henry Lee Summer band were Rick Bennick, John Cascella, John Gunnell, Debbie Lisotto, singer Mimi Mapes, Michael Organ and Michael Read.

SWEETWATER

MIKE BERRY
PERRY CHOATE
RAY CHOATE
ROCKY GIVANS
LARRY GOSHEN

Not to be confused with the national group Sweetwater, this band was formed in 1980 in Indianapolis and played the local night club scene. Sweetwater played a mixture of music that borders on country and top 40 rock & roll. In the 1990s, singer Mike Berry recorded one CD single which included Sweetwater's musicians Perry Choate, Larry Goshen and guest violinist Cathy Morris. The band performed at Bob's Midway in Greenwood for many years. Other members of the group included, Marden Baker, Gary Coan, Paul Hutchinson, Gary Jacobsen and John Shaver.

SWEETWATER (1985)
Left to right: Mike Berry – Rocky Givans – Larry Goshen – Ray Choate – Perry Choate

CRYSTAL TALIEFERO

Crystal Taliefero was born in Gary and first started performing at the age of eleven. While in her early teens, she performed with her brother in the group Magic Mist. This group opened for such acts as The Staple Singers, Deniece Williams and Gladys Knight and the Pips. While attending Indiana University, she joined a band entitled Kilo, and then was recruited by John Mellencamp for the national "Scarecrow" tour. While touring in Los Angeles, she was spotted by singer Bob Seger. After the Mellencamp tour was completed, she joined him to perform saxophone, percussion and contribute to background vocals. Crystal later returned to Bloomington in 1987 to perform on John Mellencamp's album "The Lonesome Jubilee."

THRUST

TIM BERRY
STEVE DELONG
MARK GALSTER
CURT ROBINETTE
MIKE SULLIVAN

This top 40 band was formed in the mid-1980s. They performed original material earning them popularity on the nightclub circuit. They entertained at the Vogue in Indianapolis, and toured throughout the Midwest.

TOXIC REASON

TERRY HOWE
ROB LUCJAK
J.J. PEARSON
ED PITTMAN
GREG STORT
BRUCE STUCKLEY

This punk-origin rock band from the Indianapolis area recorded several albums in the 1980s before disbanding in 1991. Recordings include "Independence" (1982) on Risky-Bitzcore, "Kill By Remote Control" (1984) Alternative Tentacles, "Within These Walls" (1985) Treason, "Bullets For You" (1986) Alternative Tentacles and "Dedication 1979-1988" (1988) on Funhouse.

VOICES

DAVE DERRIKSON
BRYAN DISBRO
ELLIOTT JACKSON
BILLY MERCURY
WANDA MICHELI
DALLAS MILLER
RUSTY SAPP

Formed in 1983, this Indianapolis band worked the nightclub circuit and performed top 40 and original material. Other members of this group were Rick Alexander and Joe Bishop.

WHY ON EARTH

MARK CUTSINGER
DWAYNE KENDALL
MICKEY MACE
JASON STONEWALL
JOE JOE WEEKEND

This Indiana group was formed in the mid-1980s. They recorded one LP self-titled "Why On Earth" (1985).

WHY ON EARTH

WILDFIRE

MIKE BERRY
DAVE ELMORE
PAUL HUTCHINSON
GARY JACOBSEN
JACKIE JACOBSEN
BILL KIRKPATRICK
DAVE MARTIN
JOHN SCOTT

This short-lived band was formed in 1985. They were finalists in the Marlboro Country Music Contest of the same year.

WILDFIRE (1985)
Left to right: John Scott – Paul Hutchinson – Dave Elmore – Gary Jacobsen – Dave Martin – Jackie Jacobsen (Not pictured, Bill Kirkpatrick and Mike Berry.)

Let the Good Times Roll

The Naughty Nineties

Let the Good Times Roll

The Naughty Nineties

The Bill Clinton era pervaded the persona of the 1990s. The unlikely successor to George Bush became a controversial president whose regime would be rocked with personal scandal. Regardless, he became the only sitting president to play the saxophone!

Prior to Clinton's residence in the White House, George Bush dueled with Iraqi madman Saddam Hussein. After Saddam decided Kuwait was to his liking and invaded the country, Bush countered with American might in the Gulf War. Superior firepower permitted Bush to win, but he never snuffed out Saddam. He would continue to be a thorn in the side of the United States for the remainder of the decade and beyond.

America's previous archenemy, the Soviet Union, became embattled in economic strife and relations thawed as new countries in that region were established. In the United States, the economy flourished and millions became wealthy through investment in the Internet. The term, "Dot-Comers" was added to the vocabulary to indicate those who believed that cyberspace was the space of the future.

Films that were popular as the '90s began included *Dick Tracy*, *Teenage Mutant Turtles*, and *Good Fellas*. *Married With Children* became a wacky way for television viewers to view the modern family.

On the music scene, rap music was the rage and new groups like Boyz II Men and Spice Girls became popular. Madonna recordings topped the charts and Michael Jackson and John Mellencamp continued to be headliners. The jazz world lost icons such as Miles Davis, Art Blakey, Gerry Mulligan, and Stan Getz. The rock n' roll world mourned the passing of the gravelly voice disc jockey, Wolfman Jack. Stephen King novels such as *Misery* scared the bejesus out of readers. John Grisham books sold millions. Golfer Tiger Woods became a phenomenon.

Popular songs in the '90s included Whitney Houston's, "I Will Always Love You," MC Hammer's, "You Can't Touch This," "Ice Ice Baby," "Man In The Box," by Alice In Chains, "November Rain" by Guns N' Roses, and "Black or White" by Michael Jackson.

Since the 1990s produced so many different forms of music, Indiana musicians that recorded them vary as much as the type of clothes and hair styles that filtered through the decade. One Indiana born and bred musician who made his mark was Kenneth "Babyface" Edmonds. His creative talent as a songwriter and producer boosted the careers of many artists. Others who contributed to the music scene included Cathy Morris, the popular jazz violinist who played fusion jazz/rock as well as Latin and classical.

Nightspots that heralded Indiana performers included the Patio and the Vogue as well as the Cozy, C.T. Peppers, and the Rathskeller. Jazz clubs such as the Chatterbox and the Jazz Kitchen were quite popular. Outdoor venues such as Deer Creek, the Circle Fest, the Mid-summer Fest, and Indiana's first national festival, the Indy Jazz Fest, flourished.

The 1990s was a "musical fest" famous for variety and new voices. Indiana musicians continued to play their part on the national and international scene. Included among those who performed during **The Naughty Nineties** were:

BABYFACE (KENNETH EDMONDS)

Kenneth Edmonds was born in Indianapolis, Indiana on April 10, 1959. He began his music career in the 1970s with the Indiana group "Manchild." He later joined his two brothers Kevon and Melvin in their R&B band, "After 7," and the Cincinnati group "Steele" with producing partner, Antonio "L.A." Reid. Although most of his solo recording work is excellent, Baby Face is most recognized for his achievements as a producer. By 1997, he earned one hundred and sixteen top 10 R&B and pop hits, with 46 of them topping the R&B charts. One of Edmond's productions, "End of the Road" by Boyz II Men, stayed at number one on the Billboard charts for 13 weeks. With partner Reid, he produced hits for such artists as Toni Braxton, Bobby Brown, Whitney Houston, Boyz II Men, Eric Clapton, Brandy, Madonna and many others. To honor Edmonds, a stretch of I-65 southeast of Indianapolis is named for him.

THE BEAUTIFUL AUTHENTIC ZOO GODS

ANTHONY COOPER
SCOTT DAVIS
ERIC GRIMMITT
LEWIS S. JONES
JEFF KETRON

This Indianapolis-based band recorded a CD entitled "Birth" (1993) on the Los Angles record label, CLEOPATRA.

MIKE BERRY

Indianapolis singer/guitarist Mike Berry performed with the Sweetwater band in the mid-1980s. After twelve years with Sweetwater, Berry recorded a CD single featuring violinist Cathy Morris. Entitled "If We Were Gypsy's,"

CATHY MORRIS & MIKE BERRY
(Photograph by Larry Goshen)

Let the Good Times Roll

this 2-song CD was recorded on Renee' Records. The title track was written and produced by drummer Larry Goshen. The second song "Don't Ever Love Me Like This" was penned by Mike Berry.

BIRDMEN OF ALCATRAZ

DINO CODALATA (GOOGOOMA)
RUSS JOHNSON (CHOC)
MATTHEW VAN KERSEN (SKYSKRAPA)
STEVE WOLF (PAPPAW)

This Indianapolis rock band was formed in the 1990s. They recorded a song on the Surf Record label entitled "Focus" (1996).

BLAQ LILY

Blaq Lily was formed in 1999 by the husband and wife team of Arminta and Raven. Arminta is a native of Lafayette, and Raven was born in Laurel, Indiana. Blaq Lily derived from the folk group Special Forces, and the gothic project entitled LivingDead. This neo-celtic acoustic duo performs in Indianapolis and the surrounding area. They recorded their first CD in 1999 entitled Blaq Lily, and thereafter released two more recordings.

BLAQ LILY

PHIL T. BLUES

From Kokomo, Phil Thompson recorded one CD, "The Original Kokomo Bluesman," in 1996. He performed on the nightclub circuit in Kokomo, as well as the popular Slippery Noodle in Indianapolis. Phil began his music career by performing with the group Heavy in the mid-1960s.

PHIL T. BLUES

BLIND OTIS & THE LOST HIGHWAY

JEFF DOWNEY
DAVE HOOPER
NICK SWEET RIVER JONES
BLIND OTIS

This Indiana R&B blues band recorded one CD, "Fools Parade" (1996) on Freedom Machine Records.

TIM BRICKLEY

TIM BRICKLEY

Indianapolis-based Tim Brickley moved from San Francisco to Indiana in the mid-1970s. A graduate of North Central High School and Indiana University, Brickley became highly successful as a composer, performer and producer. He performed in the mid-1980s with Today's Icons and opened for such acts as Culture Club. With his New York composing partner David Rheins, he produced the CD, "Be Apart," (1995). This recording featured Brickley with the Bleeding Hearts, a rock band formed in Indianapolis. In 1998, Brickley won an Emmy Award (Outstanding Achievement in Musical Composition) for his score of the documentary Hoosier Hoops: The Golden Era. His song "Tangled and Tempted" was featured in the 1998 film release of "Going All The Way." Brinkley is well known for his jazz vocalizing with the Tim Brinkley Quintet. He continues to perform at music venues in the Indiana area. Members of the Bleeding Hearts include Kevin Anker, Tad Armstrong, John Byrne and Steve Prince.

BUZZY JONES

STEVE BUTCHER
GREG HEDGES
RICHARD OWENS

BUZZY JONES

This Indianapolis-based band recorded several CD's, including "Buzzy Jones" (1993) on Hipswervy Records, "Female Delight" (1995) and "To Helmsburg And Back" (1996) on Billy Boy Records.

Let the Good Times Roll

LARRY CALLAND (CONGA JAZZ)

Percussionist Larry Calland was originally from Toledo, Ohio, but called Indianapolis his home since the mid-1990s. He performed briefly with the groups Beeble Brox, and The Drums of West Africa. In the mid-1990s, Calland formed the group Conga Jazz. That group performed at local concerts, and popular nightclubs such as the Chatterbox and Jazz Kitchen. In 1999, he recorded the CD "Spirit." Conga Jazz included musicians Robert Coleman, Dr. Virginia Jefferson, Bill Myers and saxophonist Kenny Kipp.

LARRY CALLAND

JAN ALDRIDGE CLARK

Jan Aldridge Clark was born and raised in Detroit, Michigan, but resided in Indianapolis. The variety of Clark's musical ability as a harpist, including the ability to play jazz, separates her style from others. She performed with her jazz trio at the popular Chatterbox. She can be heard on Keni Washington's recording of "Erosonata."

JAN ALDRIDGE CLARK
Photograph by Larry Goshen

Let the Good Times Roll

GOVERNOR DAVIS & THE BLUES AMBASSADORS

RON "R.C." COFFMAN
GOVERNOR DAVIS
JOSE C. JOVEN
STEVE ROBBINS

GOVERNOR DAVIS

Originally from Chicago, Governor Davis calls Indianapolis his home. His first musical influences came from his father. He performed in Chicago's north-side nightclubs. Davis studied keyboards and received gospel influences from his Aunt Ollie, a church organist. The Blues Ambassadors performed a mixture of soul and R&B. In 1997, they recorded a CD entitled, "I Am The Governor."

KARA DAY

Indiana native Kara Day has been performing the violin since she was four years old. She has performed locally and nationally with such groups as the Indianapolis Symphony Orchestra, the Philharmonic of Fort Wayne and New Jersey, the Long Island Philharmonic, the New York Pops and the American Jazz Philharmonic. Kara has backed up such national acts as Elton John, James Taylor, Natalie Cole, Led Zeppelin and Sting, and has recorded with such local artists as Cathy Morris, Frank Glover and Cynthia Layne & Leta Essig. Kara Day is not only an accomplished violinist, but also a singer and writer who has performed and fronted her own rock band.

KARA DAY
Photograph by Larry Goshen

Let the Good Times Roll

GENE DEER

Blues singer Gene Deer was born and raised in Indianapolis. Deer began playing guitar at the age of twelve. By the age of fourteen, he was performing for friends in his neighborhood. He launched his professional career at age sixteen. In the mid-1980s, Deer performed with the rock band "Coda, and in 1989 "The Generators." In 1993 Deer won fourth place in the B.B. King National Blues Competition, and in 1995 recorded his first CD "Soul Tender." His latest recording, "Livin With The Blues" (1998) was released on the SLIPPERY NOODLE label.

GENE DEER
Photograph by Larry Goshen

JENNIE DE VOE

Muncie, Indiana native Jennie DeVoe was raised in a musical family. While being nurtured by that environment, she entered the world of entertainment. After working with the Larry Crane band (John Mellencamp's guitarist), and the "No Regrets" blues group, Jennie recorded voice-overs for radio commercials. In 1998, her original song "Red Hot Sun" was chosen Honorable Mention in the John Lennon Songwriting Contest. In 1999, she made a personal appearance with Dick Clark, and was inducted into the American Bandstand Hall of Fame. Jennie has recorded two CD's under her own name, "Does She Walk On Water," and "Ta Da," both on the Rubin The Cat label.

JENNIE DE VOE
Photograph by Larry Goshen

Let the Good Times Roll

DOG TALK

MICHAEL BECK
CLIFF FORTNEY
BILL LANCTON
JIM LITCHFIELD
CLIFF WHITE

DOG TALK

Indianapolis group Dog Talk performs a unique blend of World Music—calypso, pop, reggae, rock, Latin and zydeco. They have performed in clubs around the Midwest. Dog Talk has opened for such acts as Bonnie Raitt, Bruce Hornsby, Phish, and Buckwheat Zydeco. Their debut CD titled, "It Happens Every Day"(1995), was recorded live at the popular Indianapolis club, the Jazz Kitchen.

STEVE DOKKEN

Steve Dokken is well known in the Midwest as one of the finest bass musicians. Raised in Minneapolis, Dokken moved to Indianapolis in the late 1970s. He performed with Henry Mancini from 1979 until Mancini's death in 1994. Dokken has performed with Rod Stewart, Moody Blues, Natalie Cole, Johnny Mathis and many others. Through the latter part of the 1990s and early 2000s, Steve Dokken recorded and performed with popular jazz violinist Cathy Morris.

STEVE DOKKEN
Photograph by Larry Goshen

DRAMA QUEEN

BEAU BRINKLEY
JULIE GERARD
BEA ISAACS
PAM LEE
KELLY OLIVER

This all-girl group performed in the 1980s under the name of The Girls.

In 1999, after re-forming (with all original members), they have become one of Indiana's most popular all-female bands. Their latest recording self-titled "Drama Queen" has received much airplay in the Hoosier State.

DRAMA QUEEN

LETA ESSIG

Indianapolis-born singer Leta Essig has performed in many theater stage productions, including the popular Footlight Musicals. She recorded backup voice for many artists, including the final release of the late Bobby Helms. Leta performed a long stint with the popular group Trinia & The Gypsies. In 1999, she teamed up with singer Cynthia Layne for the showcase album, "Just For A Thrill." She lives in the Indianapolis area and performs with the band Sequel.

RONNIE HAIG BAND & THE PLETCHERS

GILBERT GORDON
LARRY GOSHEN
RONNIE HAIG
PAUL HUTCHINSON

(THE PLETCHERS)
CARLA SUE PLETCHER
ROXIE PLETCHER

This showcase group became the first house band and opening act at the Fountain Room, located in the historic Fountain Square Theatre building in Indianapolis. The Fountain Room opened in 1994. It showcased the sounds of the 1950s and 60s. This band featured recording artist Ronnie Haig and back up singers, sisters

LETA ESSIG
Photograph by Larry Goshen

Left to right: Roxie Pletcher – Carla Sue Pletcher – Ronnie Haig
Photograph by Larry Goshen

Roxie and Susie Pletcher. Roxie is an accomplished songwriter. Keyboardist and singer Carla Sue (Susie) is married to Haig, and is an assistant in his home recording studio. The band previously featured keyboardist Gilbert Gordon, who released his own CD "Double Or Nothin" in 1997, and saxophonist Paul Hutchinson, whose recording of "Saxy Moods," was released in 1998. (Information on Ronnie Haig can be found in the 1950s section).

RONNIE HAIG BAND (1994)
Left to right (top): Ronnie Haig – Gilbert Gordon – Paul Hutchinson
(front): Larry Goshen

MONIKA HERZIG & PETER KIENLE (BEEBLE BROX)

Monika and Peter were born and raised in Germany, but moved to the United States around 1988. They have been permanent residents of Bloomington since 1991. Monika holds a Masters Degree in Music Education from the University of Alabama and a Doctorate in Music Education and Jazz Studies from Indiana University. Peter composes and arranges music and the two

MONIKA HERZIG
Photograph by Larry Goshen

Let the Good Times Roll

lead the popular Bloomington jazz-fusion group, Beeble Brox. They have released several recordings including "Entropy" (1990), "The Thing" (1991), "Raw Material" (1994), "Quantumn Tweezers" (1995), "Indianapolis Intergalactic Spaceport" (1997) and "Dominanc Domain" (1998). Peter also performed guitar on the Acme release, "3rd Man" (1998), with musicians Jack Helsley and Pete Wilhoit. Monika released a CD in 2000, entitled "Monika Herzig Acoustic Project, Melody Without Words."

PETER KIENLE
Photograph by Larry Goshen

KEVIN JOHNSON

Drummer Kevin Johnson was born in Brooklyn on April 22, 1951. Kevin's father is J. J. Johnson, one of the world's greatest jazz trombonists. Living in a musical family, Kevin began playing drums when he was six years old. He later performed for five years with Les McCann, and made several recordings. Kevin toured with his father's band, and in the mid-1980s moved to Indianapolis. He performs regularly with his own band, and fills in on drums with groups led by Oliver Nelson Jr., Michael Brown and many others.

CYNTHIA LAYNE

Cynthia Layne was born in Dayton, Ohio, but has been a resident of Indianapolis for many years. A singer of jazz, soul, pop and r&b, Cynthia has appeared at some of Indy's top nightclubs. They include The Jazz Kitchen, the Chatterbox and many

KEVIN JOHNSON
Photograph by Larry Goshen

Let the Good Times Roll

well-known clubs in Chicago and Cincinnati. In 1999, Layne recorded a showcase CD with singer Leta Essig entitled "Just For A Thrill," on Face The Music Records. In 2001, Cynthia released a CD entitled "In Due Time." She now fronts her own band, "Cynthia Layne & Friends."

MA KELLEY

COZY JOHNSON
DAN METRO
TERRY POTTS
TROY SEELE
BO WALLACE

This Indianapolis band recorded five albums in the 1990s on the Surf Record label. Some were released on vinyl. Later recordings were pressed on CD. The recordings included the self-titled "Ma Kelley," "Some Live, Some Not," "Banned In America," "Change In The Weather" and "Human Dance."

CYNTHIA LAYNE
Photograph by Larry Goshen

ANN McWILLIAMS

Singer-songwriter Ann McWilliams was born in Indianapolis and graduated from Lawrence Central High School. She appeared on the nationally televised *Jenny Jones show*, and hosted her own radio program *The City of Music Radio Hour*. She recorded and performed in the mid-1980s with Plaid Descent, and later released two CD's under her own name "Ann McWilliams" (1999), and "Sister Luna & The Diamond Stars" (2001).

ANN McWILLIAMS
Photograph by Larry Goshen

Let the Good Times Roll

MIKE MILLIGAN & STEAM SHOVEL

BOB BRIETUNG
BRETT DONOVAN
BARRY KEM
MIKE MILLIGAN
Earlier members were:
ERIC BROWN & PATRICK GLASS

This Kokomo-based band was originally formed at Ball State University around 1993. Leader Mike Milligan was born and raised in Kokomo, and began playing guitar at the age of six. His father, Big Mike Milligan, was also a musician. He performed with the band Ramm, who opened for such national groups as the Drifters. Mike Milligan recorded one CD in 1998 entitled "All My Life" on the Milligan Music label.

DAVID MORGAN

Born in Indianapolis, David Morgan has been involved in music since the early 1960s. During his time as a music instructor for IUPUI, he performed regularly at the popular blues club, the Slippery Noodle. Morgan's recordings include "I Never Knew She Was Married" (1993), "Pig Trader Blues" (1995), recorded with Yank Rachell. And "How Long Must I Wait For You" (1997).

CATHY MORRIS

Columbus, Indiana native Cathy Morris is one of the top jazz violinists in the country. After earning a degree from Indiana University in violin, she became successful as a performer and bandleader. Cathy has performed with such artists as David Baker, David Darling, Darol Anger and many others. Performing with her own band she has toured Japan, played for President Bill Clinton, and recorded five CD's under her own name. Cathy's recordings include "Cathy Morris," (1993) "On The Run" (1994), "It's About Time" (1997), "A Cathy Morris Christmas" (1998), and her latest release "Welcome To My World" (2001). She

CATHY MORRIS
Photograph by Larry Goshen

can be heard on "Myths For A New Millennium" (1999), Winton Reynolds CD, "Circles In Time" (2000), and Cynthia Layne and Leta Essig's recording of "Just For A Thrill" (1999).

THE MYSTERIES OF LIFE

TINA BARBIERI
GERALDINE HAAS
FREDA LOVE
JAKE SMITH

A Bloomington-based band that recorded one CD, "Keep A Secret" (1996), for the RCA record label.

NO REGRETS

WES BEAM
STEVE BROWN
JEROME MILLS
KIM SCHILLING

This Indianapolis-based band was very popular in the 1990s. At one time, they featured popular singer and recording artist, Jennie DeVoe.

OLIVE LUCY

AARON DISTLER
ANDREW FISH
BRANDON GIBSON
JOSH GIBSON
LEO KEMPF
MAT CARTIN
AMY PENROD
ROBERT RENOCK

Evansville, Indiana-based Olive Lucy recorded one CD, self-titled "Olive Lucy" (1998), on Higher Step Records.

PLAID DESCENT

MARK BERTRAM
DIANE FERGUSON
ANN McWILLIAMS
DAVE PLEISS

Plaid Descent was formed in 1993 in Indianapolis. This group featured two female singers/guitarists, Diane Ferguson and Ann McWilliams. Recordings include two CD's, "The Loud Quiet Ones" (1993) and "Plaid Descent" (1995).

PLAID DESCENT

PUSH DOWN & TURN

JASON BARTH
TAY BOURQUEIN
JASON BROWN
MATT DEVORE
SAM KING

In the early 1990s, this band was formed in Greencastle at DePauw University. Push Down & Turn has performed more then 1,600 performances, including the H.O.R.D.E. tour. They appeared on the main stage of the X-Fest, at Verizon Wireless Music Center in Noblesville. For over ten years as performing as close friends, they have recorded four albums, and continue to tour and entertain in the Midwest.

JES RICHMOND

PHIL JACOBY
JOEY MEANS
JES RICHMOND
VICKY RICHMOND
JOHN SMOTHERMAN

This Shelbyville, Indiana band featured Shelbyville native Jes Richmond, and Vicky Richmond, originally from the St. Louis area. Jes performed nationally in Los Angeles and Denver, opening for such acts as Willie Nelson, Emmy Lou Harris, Jann Browne and the Desert Rose Band. Vicky has appeared in several movies, and performed roles in television's *Dinah,*

JES RICHMOND

General Hospital, and *Moonlighting.* The groups CD, "Full Circle" was released in 1996. It has received national airplay.

ROADHOUSE

CRAIG BLATTNER
ERIC BLATTNER
JEFF GILL
KURTIS HIGGINS
DOUG MC COY
MICHAEL MC FARLAND
BILL RITTER
PAUL SCHAFER
EZRA TODD SHELTON

Drummer Kurtis Higgins formed Roadhouse in 1990. They performed cover tunes and original material at such clubs as the Slippery Noodle, and the Cozy in Indianapolis. In 2000, Roadhouse recorded a live CD entitled "No Guarantees." It was recorded live at Mickey's Irish Pub in Carmel.

ROADHOUSE

Let the Good Times Roll

ROZEN BOMBS

TOM BEVEN
JETTA CRUSE
LISA REIMER

This band featured three talented musicians, Evansville's guitarist Tom Beven, who performed with the groups C.O.D. and Quixotic Swordfish, Paducah, Kentucky's Jetta Cruse, a keyboardist, vocalist and bassist who got her start from her family's group, The Singing Cruses, and Ludington, Michigan native Lisa Reimer, who performed drums and vocals and cites her influences as Buddy Rich and Neil Peart. They recorded one CD, "Like A Vaudeville Torpedo" (1997).

ROZEN BOMBS

SINDACATO

FRANK DEAN
CARL LoSASSO
JON MARTIN
GARY WASSON

The Indianapolis-based group Sindacato is best known as a "hillbilly soul band." That accounts for the airplay of their recordings on country and blues stations across the Midwest. The band was commended for their 1995 release of "Appalachian Pipeline." It featured fiddle and mandolin player Jason Roller and musicians Rory Harper, Allen Stratyner and Mark Kurkowski. Other known members of this group were Jim Crismore, Ralph Jeffers and Charlie Overton. Sindacato has opened for such acts as Emmylou Harris, George Jones, Todd Rundgren, Lynyrd Skynyrd and the Mavericks. They have performed for capacity audiences at Deer Creek and the Vogue in Indianapolis. In 1998 the group released their second CD, self-titled "Sindacato," on Union Records.

SMALL TALK

JIM ALBRECHT
JOZELL CARTER
CLIFFORD RATLIFF
GARY WALTERS
DAVID YOUNG

This popular Indianapolis trio/quintet was formed from the 1980s jazz group, Speakeasy. In 1995, Small Talk headlined local concerts, and performed in some of Indiana's top jazz clubs. Their CD, "In Spite Of It All" (1995) was recorded on the Forum Record label. This recording featured original compositions by saxophonist David Young and keyboardist Gary Walters.

SMALL TALK
Left to right: Jim Albrecht – Jozell Carter – Gary Walters

CHARLIE SMITH

CHARLIE SMITH

Guitarist/composer Charlie Smith was born in Anderson. He studied guitar at age sixteen. In the early 1970s, he formed the band Sojourn. In the 70s, he became a member of the group Jubal. Smith performed with Carl Storie & The Tornados in the 1980s. In the mid-1990s, he was a member of the jazz-fusion group, Timeout. Smith has performed with the Bob & Tom band. In 1997, he appeared at the Montreux Jazz Festival with pianist Steve Allee. In 1999, he released the CD, "Absolutely." It was named "Best Smooth Jazz CD" by *Nuvo Magazine*.

FRANK STEANS

Guitarist/singer Frank Steans was born in Chicago, Illinois, and raised in Anderson, Indiana. A longtime resident of Indianapolis,

Frank entertained for more then thirty years by touring the country and performing with artists such as Marvin Gaye, The Staple Singers, The Dramatics and Milly Jackson. He performs regularly with the Clifford Ratliff jazz band at such clubs as the Jazz Kitchen.

RODNEY STEPP

Rodney Stepp was born in Indianapolis and graduated from Crispus Attucks High School. He first studied piano at age thirteen. At fifteen, he was performing for the Spinners. Rodney opened for many major acts and performed at the famous Cotton Club in Chicago, Illinois. He has been musician and conductor for Atlantic recording artists, The Spinners, Sister Sledge and Ronnie Dyson. Rodney's achievements include film soundtracks, commercials, recording productions and many awards. In 1997, he released the CD Rodney Stepp & BSB, "Steppin' Out," on the Brooks Street Music label.

DARREN STROUD

Accomplished guitarist Darren Stroud was born in Orleans, Indiana. Stroud performed with musicians Yun Hui, Red Beans and Rice and his own band The Darren Stroud Excursion. With the Excursion, Stroud opened for artist's Ted Nugent, Bad Company and REO Speedwagon. Darren Stroud's guitar work can be heard on the Red Beans and Rice recordings, and on "Guitarboy Plays the Blues"

RODNEY STEPP

FRANK STEANS
Photograph by Larry Goshen

Let the Good Times Roll

(1999) and "Guitar Absolute" (2000) for the Yuni Vision label. Before moving to California in 2001, Stroud performed and recorded with Yun Hui in the techno rock group, Meme.

DARREN STROUD EXCURSION
Left to right: Glen Hopkins – Tom Hunt – Darren Stroud
Photograph by LarryGoshen

TIMEOUT

KEVIN KAISER
BARRY KETTERY
CHRIS PYLE
CHARLIE SMITH
MICHAEL STRICKLIN
GARY WALTERS

This short-lived jazz/fusion group was one of the best in the Indianapolis area in the 1990s. It featured saxophonist Michael Stricklin, keyboardist Gary Walters, and guitarist Charlie Smith. They recorded one CD entitled "Kindred Spirits" (1994).

TRANSPORTATION

ANTHONY COOPER
MARK CUTSINGER
SCOTT DAVIS
ERIC GRIMMET
ANGIE WALKER

This Bloomington-based band emerged from the group, The Beautiful Authentic Zoo Gods. Transportation seemed destined for stardom, but due to unexplained circumstances disbanded. Their lone release was "Transportation," recorded for Flat Earth Records in 1995.

TRINIA COX

TRINIA & THE GYPSIES

TRINIA COX
LETA ESSIG
CATT SADLER
JENNIFER SPARKS

THE GYPSIES
Left to right: Leta Essig – Jennifer Sparks – Catt Sadler

Indianapolis-native Trinia Cox' grandfather was an authentic Romanian gypsy. He and her violin-playing grandmother were both traditional with their song and dance. Trinia began playing piano at age eleven, and later switched to flute. She studied theater and speech at Marion College in Indianapolis. Her first professional position was with the Jamaican Reggae band, Quazar. Trinia sang and performed flute at popular nightspots such as The Vogue and The Patio. She graduated from Roosevelt University's Chicago School of Music with a Bachelor of Fine Arts degree in Music. In 1991 she moved to Los Angeles and performed in television. After returning to Indianapolis in the early 1990s, she pursued a singing position with the group Rock Doll. In 1996, Trinia formed The Gypsies (a high-octane show group) consisting of several singers and dancers. Their vocalizing and choreography filled the stage with excitement. Trinia and the Gypsies perform in the Indiana area, and anticipate their first recording.

THE VULGAR BOATMEN

ERIK BEAADE
DALE LAWRENCE
ANDY RICHARDS
MATT SPEAK
(ROBERT RAY)

The Indianapolis-based group The Vulgar Boatmen descended from the band Right to Left. Formed by leader Dale Lawrence and Florida musician Robert Ray, this group was two bands with the same name, performing in Indianapolis and the southern portion of the United States. They recorded three albums between 1989 and 1995 that received rave reviews in the United States and Europe. Two of their recordings include "You And Your Sister" (1989) on the Record Collect label, and "Please Panic" (1992) on Safehouse/ Rough Trade.

YUN HUI
Photograph by Larry Goshen

YUN HUI

Vocalist, keyboardist, performer and composer Yun Hui was born in Kangwon Do, South Korea. She moved to the United States when she was seven. Raised in Columbus, she was classically trained on piano and violin. She became popular in the music business by promoting, producing, and fronting her own band, Red Beans and Rice. She was video jockey for *Jazzbox*, a syndicated jazz television show, and developed a one-hour all-original Hoosier artist radio program on WICR 88.7 in Indianapolis. Yun Hui is featured on "Red Beans & Rice, Staples" (1993), Red Beans & Rice, Eat Big"(1996), Red Beans & Rice, Yes We Can"(1999) and her debut as a single artist, "Yun Hui, Disoriental" (2000). Yun Hui lives in Hollywood California, and is currently performing with guitarist Darren Stroud.

Let the Good Times Roll

1990 NOTABLES

ALLIGATOR BROTHERS
AMY STEPHENS
APRIL HOLBROOK
BEKI BRINDLE
BERNARD WHITTINGTON
BETH DAVIS
BIGGER THAN ELVIS
BILL LANCTON
BLACKBONE
BOA
BRENDA WILLIAMS
CARL HINES
CATHI NORTON
CHOOCH & ENCHANTERS
CHRONIC REALITY
CORN BROTHERS
DALLAS MILLER
DANE CLARK
DARIN PATRICK
DAVE & RAE
DEAD MISTER SUNSHINE
DESTINATION EARTH
DIREWOLF
FAMBOOEY
FANCY LIZARDS
GORDON BONHAM
GREG SANSING
GREGG BACON
HARVEY & THE BLUETONES
JANIECE JAFFE
JD & THE 'OL #7 BAND
JEFF DEHERDT
JENNIFER KIRK
JOHN SHAVER
JOE JACKSON
JOHNNY SOCKO
KARA BARNARD
KENI WASHINGTON
LEGENDARY FIREBIRDS
MEDICINE WHEEL
MICHAEL BROWN
MICHAEL KELSEY
MOJO HAND
MONICA CANTRELL
OLIVER SYNDROME
PAUL HOLDMAN

PURE GOLD
RADIO FLYERS
RASTABILLY REBELS
REGGIE GRIFFIN
RHETT McDANIEL
ROB SWAYNIE
RUSTY BLADEN
SAM GIBSON
SCOTT GREESON
SITUATION GREY
SUZANNE GLASS
THE BLUE MOON BOYS
THE COOLER KINGS
THE KELLY JAY ORCH.
THE MARY JANES
THE REMAINDERS
THE SHADE
THE SPIRTLES
THE WHY STORE
TONY MEDEIROS
YANK RACHELL

Let the Good Times Roll

Country and Western Guys and Gals

Let the Good Times Roll

Country

music mirrors the soul of Indiana like a good plate of grits. Those who love the sound of country crooners appreciate the music since they believe the lyrics reflect the very essence of everyday life. Most important, they say, the listener can, unlike other forms of modern music, actually understand the words.

Indiana's contribution to country music spreads a wide tablecloth. Famed entertainers such as Janie Fricke, Crystal Gayle, Sylvia, and Steve Wariner are most prominent, but artists such as Lattie Moore, Country Cousin Chickie, Charlie Gore, Charlie Stewart and Kim Crowley, all with ties to the Hoosier State, make their mark as well.

Television and radio stations flourished with country music in the 1950s. WIBC radio host Jack Morrow performed his morning Country Carnival program with guest artists Country Cousin Chickie and the Haymakers. Radio station WGEE, featuring disc jockey D.C. Mullins, was popular.

WFBM television and radio produced such shows as Indiana Hoedown, featuring Charlie Gore, Herb and Kay, and the Swanee River Boys. Charlie Gore, a West Virginian and adopted Hoosier, lived in Indianapolis for many years. A former NBC network performer, Gore recorded for the famous King label.

The Indiana Hoedown featured The Rangers. They provided background music for performers such as Lee Jones and Estil McNew's Jr. Kentucky Briarhoppers. The Rangers featured Walter Brown (accordion), Bob Boyer (bass), Ralph Cook (fiddle) and Charlie Gore (guitar).

Country stars picked their guitars and bowed their fiddles at such Indiana havens as the Sherman Bar, Blakes, the Thunderbird, Wagon Wheel and the Mocking Bird Hill. The White Cloud Jamboree in Greenwood was a must for country music buffs.

Locating information about Indiana-linked country musicians is a tall task since so many have enjoyed brief success as entertainers. That doesn't deflect from the contribution they made to the country music scene. **Country Guys and Gals** include:

JANN BROWNE

Jann Browne was born in Anderson and raised nearby Shelbyville. Her grandparents were members of the Kentucky Briarhoppers. They appeared regularly on the Grand Ole Opry. Meeting country stars inspired Jann, and she learned to play piano and sing at and early age. Browne made her first personal appearance in Shelbyville performing at the local high school. In 1978, she moved to California. Two years were spent performing with the recording artists, Asleep At The Wheel. In the 1990s, Browne released one album. It contained two singles, and both reached the Billboard Charts. Recorded on the Curb label, "Tell Me Why" (1990) climbed to the #18 position, and "Louisville" peaked at #75.

Photograph left to right: Jerry Lee Williams – Jim Chenowith – Bryan Hightower – Aubrey Cagle – Jack Wagley – (Girl singer unknown) (1958)

AUBREY CAGLE

Aubrey Cagle was born in Lexington, Tennessee but moved to Indianapolis around 1955. He purchased his first guitar at the age of eleven, and performed with his own band at age seventeen. Cagle recorded "Real Cool" (1959), on the House Of Sounds label, and released "Be-Bop" and "Come Along Little Girl" (1960), both on Glee Records. Cagle changed his name to Billy Love around 1961. He recorded several songs under that name. The recordings were on the Glee Label. Although Cagle (Billy Love) never achieved national success, his friends in the music business included Carl Perkins, Elvis Presley and Ernest Tubb.

KIM CRONLEY

Indianapolis native Kim Cronley began her professional singing career when she was fourteen. In the early 1980s, Cronley played many local nightspots, including the Wreck Bar, Blake's, the Bonfire, Cowboys and Whiskey River. She sang and performed on the saxophone. In 1988, Cronley was the opening act at the Little Nashville Opry in Nashville, Indiana for Barbara Mandrell, George Jones, Tanya Tucker, Conway Twitty, Brenda Lee, Johnny Cash and many other country artists. Continuing her career in the music business, she performs with her husband J. R. Love. They continue to open for national acts at the Little Nashville Opry.

Let the Good Times Roll

KIM CRONLEY

JAN EDWARDS

Singer Jan Edwards, a versatile performer, was born in Bloomington. Performing music with a range from Billie Holiday to Patsy Cline, she displayed her musical talent in many of Indiana's top clubs. Those included the Hilton, Raddison, Omni, the Vogue and the Broadmore Country Club. In 1970, Edwards was chosen Miss Indiana. She modeled and performed in many national and local commercials. After moving to Tennessee, Edwards performed at the Grand Ole Opry. She appears with the Joe Edwards and the "Gitfiddle Review Show."

JAN EDWARDS

JOE EDWARDS

Joe Edwards was born in Stanford a few miles from Bloomington. He started his career in the early 1950s performing on Bloomington's WTTV Channel 4, and WTTS radio. He appeared on Uncle Bob Hardy's Hayloft Frolic and the Jack Noel's Happy Valley Show. When Channel 4 moved to Indianapolis, Joe performed on television with artist Shorty Sheehan. Being an accomplished guitarist and fiddle player, he performed in 1955 at the Grand Ole Opry in Nashville. Edwards later performed with country artists Martha Carson, Bill Carlisle, Grandpa Jones, Jerry Reed, Little Jimmy Dickens and Wilma Lee & Stoney Cooper. In the late 1960s, he became a staff member of the Grand Ole Opry band. Edwards performed studio recording for labels such as Mercury, Columbia, Decca, Capitol and RCA. He worked with Chet Atkins and Owen Bradley, two of Nashville's greatest producers, and

JOE EDWARDS

Let the Good Times Roll

performed on national television with Dolly Parton and Tennessee Ernie Ford. His recording career includes performing with Ferlin Husky on his 1957 hit, "Gone," and backing such artists as Webb Pierce and Bobby Helms. Joe Edwards performs in the Nashville area, and is featured in his own production, The Gitfiddle Review.

TOMMY FLINT

Tommy Flint was born Thomas Earl Flint in Dunmor, Kentucky. He moved to Indianapolis in 1954 and began playing his first guitar when he was 14. Flint played in the Indianapolis area for many years. He is well-known as one of the greatest guitar thumb-pickers in country music. He performed in the Indianapolis area with such artists as rock-a-billy Lattie Moore, Bobby Helms and Joe Edwards. In the mid-1950s, Flint opened for Elvis Presley at the Lyric Theater in Indianapolis. He also performed with such artists as Glen Campbell, Eddy Arnold, Ray Price, Merle Travis and Chet Atkins. Flint appeared on the Grand Ole Opry and the Country Music Hall Of Fame, and has won many awards for his great contribution to country music. Tommy has written and published over thirty books on instructional guitar for the Mel Bay Publications.

Photograph left to right: Hardy Day – Tommy Flint – Jimmy Skinner – Curt Gibson (1955)

Photograph left to right: Hardy Day – Tommy Flint – Lattie Moore – Curt Gibson (1955)

JANIE FRICKIE

Janie Frickie was born on December 19, 1947, in South Whitney. As a child, she was taught to play piano, organ and guitar. She performed at the local church. After graduating from Indiana University, Frickie moved to Memphis where she sang jingles and presented call letters for a local radio station. Around 1975, Janie sang backup for singers such as Tanya Tucker and Elvis Presley. In 1977, she recorded her first solo single, "What're You Doing

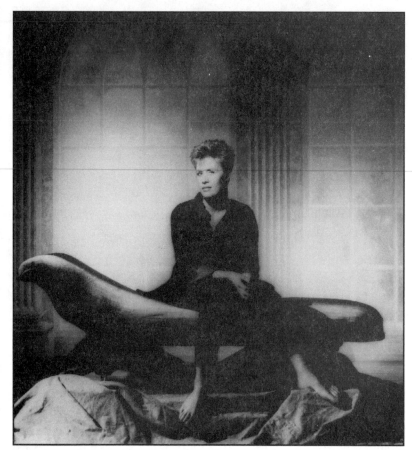

JANIE FRICKIE

Tonight," and five years later enjoyed her first big hit, "Don't Worry 'Bout Me, Baby." She later made many more hit recordings. In 1986 Frickie was named the most popular Female Solo Act by the International Country Music Awards. She is a member of the Country Music Hall of Fame.

CRYSTAL GAYLE

Crystal Gayle (Brenda Gail Webb) was born January 9, 1951 in Paintsville, Kentucky. Her family moved to Wabash, Indiana when she was just a child. Early in her career, she performed with her two sisters Loretta Lynn and Peggy Sue. At the age of sixteen, she toured with Loretta and Conway Twitty. Gayle, confident she could enter the pop scene, left to pursue her own career. In 1973, she signed with United Artists Records. Gayle was chosen, "The Most Promising Country Female Vocalist" of 1975. The album, "Must Believe In Magic," in 1977 produced her biggest pop single ever, "Don't It Make My Brown Eyes Blue." Other recognizable hits were "I'll Get Over You" (1976) and "Ready For The Times To Get Better" (1978), both recorded on United Artists Records.

HAYMAKERS

PAUL BURTON
COUNTRY COUSIN CHICKIE (CHICK HOPKINS)
TOM MORIARTY
JACK SIMPSON

This country & western band was formed in the mid-1950s. It featured fiddle, guitar, bass and accordion. A popular group in the Indianapolis area, the Haymakers performed regularly on WIBC Radio's Jack Morrows Hillbilly Hit Parade.

THE HAYMAKERS

Let the Good Times Roll

CRYSTAL GAYLE

LATTIE MOORE

Lattie Moore was not an Indiana native, but lived and performed in the Indianapolis area. Moore recorded his first song in 1952 entitled "Juke Joint Johnny" on the Speed Label. The record is very rare, and a highly sought after collector's item. It was later re-released in 1957 on the ARC label. Moore played at several country bars in Indianapolis, and for a time operated the Thunderbird Nightclub. He spent most of his recording career on the famous King Label, and had several country hits in the 1960s. They included "Cajun Doll," and "Drunk Again."   In 1961, the latter climbed to #25 in the top 100.

LATTIE MOORE

Photograph left to right: Spurs Ragsdale – Johnny Highland – Lattie Moore – Country Cousin Chickie – Patty Rindles – Bobby Phillips – Jackie Blair

Let the Good Times Roll

JACK MORROW

Disc Jockey Jack Morrow was popular in the 1950s with his country & western radio show, Hillbilly Hit Parade. Broadcast on WIBC in Indianapolis, Jack featured some live entertainment.

Photograph left to right: Country Cousin Chickie – Jack Morrow

LENNY RAY

Singer Lenny Ray, originally born in Manchester, Kentucky, moved to Indianapolis when he was twelve years old. In the mid-1950s, Lenny played the local country bars and performed in shows with artists such as Bill Monroe and Red Foley. He recorded two singles, "This Should Go On Forever/You Got Me Spinning" (1960s) and "No Man's Land/What Now?" (1970s), both on the Sweetwater Label.

LENNY RAY

RUNNING ON EMPTY

GARY BREWER
GARY JACOBSEN
JACKIE JACOBSEN
KIMMER SMITH

This country/rock band was formed around 1982 in Indianapolis. They performed in the local bar scene. Drummer Gary Brewer later performed at the Little Opry in Nashville, Indiana and opened for many national country artists. Guitarist Kimmer Smith and bassist Gary Jacobsen perform in the Indiana area. They appeared with such artists as Dolly Parton. This group also featured Jackie Jacobsen, one of Indiana's top female bass players.

RUNNING ON EMPTY (1982)
Left to right: Gary Brewer – Jackie Jacobsen
– Gary Jacobsen – Kimmer Smith

Let the Good Times Roll

Photograph left to right: Bobby Ridenour – Shorty Sergent

Let the Good Times Roll

SHORTY SERGENT

In 1958, Rock-a-Billy singer Shorty Sergent recorded a popular local hit entitled "Record Hop," on the Jet Record label. Shorty was quite popular in the country and western circuit and performed on the Indianapolis bar scene.

CONNIE SMITH

Connie Smith was born in Elkhart. She won her first amateur talent contest in the early 1960s. Guitarist Chet Atkins heard her sing and convinced Bill Anderson to write a song for her entitled, "Once A Day." It became Connie's biggest hit and was voted Song of the Year in 1964. She then reached stardom by recording such songs as "Ain't Had No Lovin'," "The Hurtin's All Over," "Baby's Back Again," "Then And Only Then," "If I Talk To Him" and "(Till) I Kissed You." In 1971, she joined the Grand Ole Opry. In 1992, Smith was inducted into the Country Music Hall Of Fame.

SYLVIA
(SYLVIA KIRBY ALLEN)

Sylvia was born in Kokomo on December 9, 1956. Her dreams of becoming a country singer began early in her childhood. After graduating from high school, she moved to Nashville, Tennessee. Sylvia recorded the song, "You Don't Miss A Thing" in 1979. It was a Billboard top 40 hit. In 1980, Sylvia recorded "Tumbleweed," a top 10 hit with RCA. Sylvia's greatest success was "Drifter" (1981). It occupied the #1 position for one week on the Billboard charts. Sylvia recorded many other songs, and later collaborated with several songwriters. She co-wrote songs for artists such as the Statler Brothers and Jimmy Fortune.

CIRCLE B RANCH GANG
Left to right: Country Cousin Chickie (Hopkins) – Paul Burton – Tom Moriarity – Ann Wagner – Dick Pittenger – Dick Green

ANN WAGNER

Born in Louisville, Kentucky, Ann Wagner was raised in Vincennes. She began on the piano and violin in grade school, and studied voice while attending the Saint Rose Academy. She began her broadcasting career in WAOV Radio in Vincennes. After moving to Indianapolis she performed nights at the Columbia Club, and days on PM Party at WIBC. In the early 1950s, Wagner was a country singer for WFBM Television's Circle B Ranch program. At that time WFBM featured both radio and television. Wagner became the first female disc Jockey in Indiana. In 1961, at the age of thirty-seven, she attended Butler University and received her master's degree. She became assistant professor for the radio and television department at Butler University in Indianapolis. In 1988, after twenty years in broadcasting, she retired from Butler University.

STEVE WARINER

STEVE WARINER

Steve Wariner was born on Christmas Day, 1954 in Noblesville. He became a successful country artist by playing bass with country stars Bob Luman and Chet Atkins. In 1971, Wariner became the bass player with the Dottie West band and remained with her until 1974. He signed with RCA in 1978, and climbed to the charts with, "All Roads Lead To You" (1981). Steve later switched to the MCA Label and continued success with "Some Fools Never Learn" (1985), Life's Highway" (1986), and "Lynda" (1987). Billed as a singer/songwriter, Steve Wariner is a hot attraction on the country & western circuit.

Let the Good Times Roll

SONNY GRUBBS & THE HOOSIER ALL-STARS (1950s)
Sonny Grubbs (top middle)
Photograph taken at the All Star Jamboree in the Lyric Theatre, Indianapolis.

Let the Good Times Roll

Let the Good Times Roll

The Jazzmakers

Let the Good Times Roll

Indiana

jazz musicians deserve a book of their own. Throughout the twentieth century, they contributed to the evolution of a type of music that embodies the very spirit of the music scene. New Orleans-bred artists such as Louis Armstrong, Al Hirt and Sidney Bechet may have birthed the sound, but Indiana artists created musical tones that enhanced the popularity of jazz.

If Indiana were to have a "Jazz Hall of Fame," the collection of artists would be never-ending. Among those who captured the hearts of jazz lovers everywhere were Wes, Monk, and Buddy Montgomery, Freddie Hubbard, Hoagy Carmichael, Slide Hampton, J. J. Johnson, and David Baker. Others such as Steve Allee, Royce Campbell, Jimmy Coe, and Alonzo "Pookie" Johnson were outstanding.

Jazz clubs were an integral part of the Indiana music arena. In the 1950s, The Sunset Terrace, The British Lounge, the 440 Club, Henri's and George's Bar flourished. Jazz musicians from around the world played at those venues and at the Pink Poodle, the Missile Club, and the Barrington Lounge.

Jazz outlets spilling out the dynamic tones of jazz include the Jazz Kitchen, owned by jazz musician David Allee. That club and proprietor David Andrichik's Chatterbox feature Indiana jazz artists and noted musicians with national and international reputations. **Jazzmakers** that have shined wherever they have performed include:

AFFINITY

This jazz/fusion group was formed in 1976. It featured original members Royce Campbell, Terry Cook, Larry King, Art Reiner and Bruce Stanforth. A later member was percussionist Kevin Kaiser. Affinity recorded one album "Around The Town" (1987), on the Raised Eyebrow label.

AFFINITY (1989)
Left to right: Larry King – Art Reiner – Kevin Kaiser
(front): Royce Campbell

DAVID ALLEE

David Allee was born March 24, 1969 in Indianapolis. The son of noted jazz pianist Steve Allee, and proprietor of the popular Jazz Kitchen, David has been an accomplished trumpet player for more than twenty years. He performs on stage with many groups, including the Jimmy Coe Big Band.

STEVE ALLEE

Indianapolis-born Steve Allee served in the 82nd Airborne Division Army Band. After a short stint with the Buddy Rich band, Steve returned to Indiana to pursue his jazz career. As a pianist and composer, he co-led the Von Ohlen-Allee Big Band with drummer John Von Ohlen. He performed at many jazz festivals including the Montreux Jazz Festival in Switzerland. Steve has written and arranged recordings for television sound tracks including The Lost World, NBC's Name Your Adventure and ABC's America's Best Kept Secrets. His recording credits are featured on the syndicated *Bob and Tom* Show as well as the recordings of other artists. Recordings under his own name include, "The Magic Hour" on

DAVID ALLEE
Photograph by Larry Goshen

Let the Good Times Roll

STEVE ALLEE

Noteworthy Records, "Mirage," and "New York In The Fifties" (1998), on the AlleeOop label.

DAVID BAKER

David Baker was born on December 21, 1931 in Indianapolis. Early in his career, he performed with jazz legends Wes Montgomery and Slide Hampton. David toured on trombone with Buddy Johnson and in 1956 performed with the Stan Kenton Orchestra. In 1957, he worked with Maynard Ferguson, and in 1961 joined the Lionel Hampton band. After a stint with Quincy Jones in 1962, a muscular disease forced Baker to concentrate on the cello. David Baker continues to be a well-known performer and educator and is chairman of the Indiana University jazz department.

Photograph left to right: Benny Barth – Frank Glover (1988)
Photograph by Larry Goshen

BENNY BARTH

Benny Barth was born on February 16, 1929 in Indianapolis. He studied tap dancing at the age of four and played the accordion and trumpet in grade school. While attending Shortridge High School, he played drums with the Barton Rogers Orchestra. Benny performed on the infamous Indiana Avenue at such nightspots as Andres, George's Bar and the Cotton Club. He performed locally with Erroll Grandy, Buddy Parker, Slide Hampton, Leroy Vinnegar, David Baker, Jimmy Coe and Freddie Hubbard. Barth was also a regular member of the Buddy and Monk Montgomery group The Mastersounds. Barth recorded thirteen albums for the World Pacific label and two for Fantasy Records. He had two recordings on the Fantasy Label with Vince Guaraldi, including the original sound track of *A Boy Named Charlie Brown*. For three years, Barth was the house drummer at the popular Hungri I in San Francisco. He performed with such artists as Barbara Streisand, Mel Torme and Jon Hendricks. Other musicians Benny recorded with include Joe Venuti, Ben Webster, Jimmy Witherspoon, Pearl Bailey and Joe Williams.

Let the Good Times Roll

JOHN BUNCH

John Bunch was born 1921 in Tipton. He began playing piano at the age
of eleven, but never played professionally until his mid-thirties. In the early
1950s, Bunch performed with Georgie Auld, and in the late 1950s played with
Woody Herman, Benny Goodman and Maynard Ferguson. From 1966 through
1972, Bunch was musical director for Tony Bennett. He also performed and
directed the Buddy Rich band.   As the leader of his own band (1975-1977), he
recorded five albums under his name.

GARY BURTON

Anderson native Gary Burton studied piano at age six. He was self-taught on
the vibes. In 1963, he toured the United States and Japan with pianist George
Shearing. In 1964, joined the Stan Getz quartet. They performed at the White
House. Burton appeared in two films, The Hanged Man and Get Yourself A
College Girl. In the late 1960s, he formed his own group with guitarist Larry
Coryell. Since 1970 he has frequently performed with Keith Jarrett and Chick
Corea.

CANDOLI BROTHERS

The Candoli Brothers Pete and Conte, were born in Mishawaka in the 1920s.
Pete performed on trumpet with top name bands such as Tommy Dorsey, Glen
Miller, Woody Herman, Stan Kenton, and Count Basie. He composed and
arranged music for Judy Garland, Ella Fitzgerald, and Peggy Lee. He also
recorded with Henry Mancini, Nelson Riddle and Quincy Jones. Brother Conte
joined the Woody Herman Band in 1945, and remained a permanent member
for ten years. He also performed with Benny Goodman, Dizzy Gillespie and
Stan Kenton. In 1954, he formed his own group with sidemen Chubby Jackson,
Frank Rosolino and Lou Levy. Conte moved to Los Angeles and for four years
joined the Lighthouse All-Stars featuring Shorty Rogers, Bud Shank and Bob
Cooper. He recorded with Gerry Mulligan, Shelly Manne, Terry Gibbs, Frank
Sinatra, Bing Crosby, Sammy Davis Jr. and Sarah Vaughan. In 1967, Conte
joined the Tonight Show starring Johnny Carson. He became a permanent
member of the Doc Severinsen Orchestra and remained with Severinsen until
Carson's retirement in 1992. The Candoli Brothers have performed and
appeared on television and in movies. Pete died December 14, 2001. Conte
continues to perform solo while occasionally appearing with Doc Severinsen.

ROYCE CAMPBELL

Since his stepfather was a naval officer, Royce Campbell, a native of Seymour, Indiana, was raised in Japan, Spain, Barbados, Pennsylvania and South Carolina. Learning to play the guitar at the age of nine, he was first influenced by blues and rock, and then jazz. After graduating from high school, Campbell moved to Indianapolis to live with his uncle, musician Carroll DeCamp. Campbell later toured with Marvin Gaye, and in 1975 began a long stint with the Henry Mancini Orchestra. Royce has performed with Richard Groove Holmes, Jack McDuff, Sarah Vaughn, Nancy Wilson, Melvin Rhyne and Joe Williams. He has recorded more than ten albums under his own name. He lives in Harrisonburg, Virginia and continues to be a successful recording artist.

ROYCE CAMPBELL (1981)

HOAGY CARMICHAEL

Born November 11, 1899, in Bloomington, Hoagy Carmichael wrote his most popular composition, "Stardust" in 1929. He composed many other great songs until his death in 1981. Active in the 1950s, Carmichael played a cameo roll in the film "A Man With A Horn," a movie based on the life of Bix Beiderbecke. In 1951, he won an Academy Award for his composition, "In the Cool, Cool, Cool of the Evening." He also recorded several albums, one with jazz legends Art Pepper and Jimmy Rowles in the 1950s. In the early '60s, Carmichael toured the United States and Europe, making solo appearances and performing on radio and television.

HOAGY CARMICHAEL
Photograph by Duncan Schiedt

Let the Good Times Roll

Hoagy Carmichael provided many great compositions including "Up The Lazy River," "Skylark," and "Georgia On My Mind."

LAWRENCE CLARK III

Lawrence Clark III grew up in Indianapolis. His family was musically inclined and he became a percussionist. He performed with some of the world's finest musicians, including Grover Washington, Richard Groove Homes, David "Fathead" Newman, and James Moody. He also played with jazz legends Jimmy Coe, Errol Grandy, Pookie Johnson and David Young. Clark is a teacher of percussion and jazz, and continues to educate and influence the young artists of today.

LAWRENCE CLARK III (1988)
Photograph by Larry Goshen

JIMMY COE

Jimmy Coe was born in Tompkinsville, Kentucky, but he has lived in Indianapolis since the late 1930s. From 1950 until 1953, Jimmy performed with his own band at the Cotton Club on Indiana Avenue. In 1953, he recorded the R&B hit, "After Hours Joint," on the State Label. Coe also recorded for the King label in Cincinnati under the name of Jimmy Cole. In the 1960s, Coe performed with the trio that included Melvin Rhyne on B3 organ and drummer Sonny Johnson. This trio entertained at clubs such as the Barrington Lounge and the Pink Poodle. Coe performed with some of the greatest jazz legends including Freddie Hubbard, J. J. Johnson, Jay McShann, Tiny Bradshaw and many others. He is well known for his "big band" sounds. In 1994, he recorded his CD, "Say What?" on Time Records. That

Photograph left to right: Jimmy Coe – Erroll Grandy (1988)
Photograph by Larry Goshen

recording was dedicated to Jimmy Mumford, who was Coe's drummer since 1970, and William "Whitey" Harris, who's last recording was that CD. Jimmy continues to perform in the Indianapolis area, playing special engagements and working in top clubs such as the Chatterbox and the Jazz Kitchen.

CAL COLLINS

Born in Medora, Indiana, Cal Collins grew up listening to country and western music. While playing guitar at the age of thirteen, he was influenced by the form of jazz. In the 1950s, he performed in a local jazz quartet. After spending two years in the Army, he settled in Cincinnati. Cal spent three years touring with the famous Benny Goodman band performing in concerts across the USA, and in Europe and Japan.

EDDIE CONDON

Eddie Condon was born in Goodland, Indiana. He became a professional jazz banjoist at the age of seventeen. Condon performed with such artists as Jimmy McParland, Bud Freeman and Red Nichols. He recorded with such jazz greats as Louis Armstrong, Jack Teagarden and Gene Krupa. In the 1950s, Eddie recorded on the Columbia label and in 1957 toured Great Britain with his own group. In 1964, he toured Australia and New Zealand. He was able to attend his own benefit concert at Carnegie Hall shortly before his death in 1973.

DAVID DARLING

David Darling was born in Elkhart on March 4, 1941. He studied piano at the age of four, and began to play the cello at age ten. He played bass and alto sax in high school and studied classical cello at Indiana University. David worked with the Paul Winter Consort from 1970 through 1978, and toured throughout the USA while recording four albums. He recorded several other albums including Ralph Towner's "Old Friends, New Friends" (1979), with Kenny Wheeler, Michael Di Pasqua and Eddie Gomez. Darling recorded in 1980 with vibraharpist Dave Samuels. In 1981, he was co-founder of a group entitled Gallery. That group successfully recorded and toured through out the USA. Darling plays both traditional cello and his self-designed eight-string solid-body. By using such attachments as an echoplex, ring modulator and a fuzz box, he plays a variety of music from traditional classic to rock and jazz.

DICK DICKINSON

Drummer Dick Dickinson was born on January 2, 1928 in Emory, Georgia. He was raised in Petersburg, Indiana. Dick played with the George Boldi Dance Orchestra from 1950 through 1951. In 1952, he performed with the Freddy Dale Orchestra. They placed second in Indiana University's National College Jazz Competition. In the mid-1950s, Dick played the local jazz clubs and performed with such artists as David Baker, Al Kiger and Jimmy Coe. From 1970 until 1972, he was producer and host for the "Explorations in Jazz" radio show on WFIU at Indiana University. His radio show "Just Jazz," was aired on WIAN from 1985 until 1986, and on WFYI Radio from 1986 until 1990. In 1985, Dick was awarded the Key to the City of Indianapolis and was later inducted into the Jazz Foundation Hall of Fame.

DICK DICKINSON

FRANK GLOVER

Frank Glover was born June 27, 1963 in Indianapolis. He attended Indiana University School of Music. His specialty is the clarinet and saxophone. Glover has performed regularly at the popular Chatterbox jazz club since he was 21. He also appears weekly at The Jazz Kitchen. Glover produced three CD's under his own name, "Mosaic" (1991), "Something Old, Something New" (1994), and the clarinet/piano duo with Claude Sifferlen "Siamese Twins," all on FGA Records. He performed at Carnegie Hall in 1996, and has also played the Chicago Jazz Festival. Frank won the 1995 National Endowment for the Arts jazz performance award.

FRANK GLOVER
Photograph by Larry Goshen

ERROLL GRANDY

Erroll Grandy (known by his friends as Groundhog), was born January 2, 1921 in Norfolk, Virginia. Erroll moved to Indianapolis in 1936. He graduated from Crispus Attucks High School. In 1942, Grandy attended Jordan's Conservatory of Music. He was partially blind, but that was no handicap, Grandy was well-known in Indianapolis as the *Godfather of Jazz*. He was considered a mentor to many local jazz musicians such as Wes Montgomery, Freddie Hubbard, Slide Hampton and J. J. Johnson. In the early 1950s, Grandy formed his own group and performed at clubs such as the Ritz Lounge and Henri's Petri Room on the fabled Indiana Avenue. In 1953, he performed with the Jimmy Coe Band, and in 1955 joined the Count Fisher Trio. Erroll Grandy died on June 12, 1991.

RAYFORD GRIFFIN

RAYFORD GRIFFIN

Rayford Griffin was born February 6, 1958 in Indianapolis. He studied drums at age thirteen. While attending Shortridge High School, he performed with a band called Tarnished Silver. That group included singer/guitarist Kenny Edmonds, better known today as Babyface. After graduating from high school, Rayford joined the band, Merging Traffic. The group opened for many name acts including Grover Washington and Jean-Luc Ponty.

In 1980, while opening for Ponty, Griffin had the chance to tour and record with the Jean-Luc Ponty band. He recorded six albums with Jean-Luc Ponty including "Mystical Adventures" (1982), "Individual Choice" (1983), "Open Mind" (1984) and "Fables" (1985) all on the Atlantic Label. "The Gift of Time" (1987) and "Storytelling" (1989) on CBS Records. Griffin has recorded with among others, Boyz ll Men, George Howard, Stanley Clarke, George Duke and Patrice Rushen. He has toured and performed with Michael Jackson, Anita Baker, The Isley Brothers, Bette Midler, Babyface, Manhattan Transfer and Cameo. A writer/singer and a drummer, he lives in California and has released his own CD entitled "Rebirth Of The Cool."

Let the Good Times Roll

SLIDE HAMPTON

Slide (Locksley) Hampton was born in Jennette, Pennsylvania, but he and his musical family moved to Indianapolis in the early 1940s. Hampton performed with Buddy Johnson in the 1950s. Between 1955 and '56, he performed with the Lionel Hampton Band. In 1957, Slide played trombone and arranged for Maynard Ferguson. From 1959 through 1962, he was musical arranger for singer Lloyd Price. Six years later, Hampton performed and toured Europe with the Woody Herman Band. In 1977, he formed his own group, "The World of Trombones." Hampton is responsible for many recordings including "Sister Salvation" (1960), "Jazz With A Twist" (1962), and "Two Sides Of Slide" (1962).

SLIDE HAMPTON
Photograph by Larry Goshen

CHERRYL HAYES

Cherryl Hayes was born in Indianapolis and graduated from Chrispus Attucks High School. She performed locally at the Jazz Kitchen and the Indy Jazz Fest. She was voted "Best Indy Jazz Vocalist" by *Nuvo Weekly Magazine.* Cherryl appeared nationally at the Oriental Hotel in Bangkok Thailand and performed for the King and Queen of Bangkok. She was featured at the Tavern on the Green in New York City. Hayes continues to perform locally and nationally.

DAVE HEPLER

Indiana-native Dave Hepler took his first piano lesson at the age of eight. He studied trumpet at age nine, and was playing professionally in his father's band by the time he

Photograph left to right: Jim Hepler – Jay Hammel – Melvin James – Joe Deal – Dave Hepler

FREDDIE HUBBARD
Photograph by Duncan Schiedt

Let the Good Times Roll

was eleven. Dave studied music at Indiana University. While living with his trumpet-playing father, he turned his main interest to jazz. Dave resides in the Indianapolis area and performs at such clubs as the Stillwater, Chatterbox, the City Taproom, and the Midtown Café. One of his earlier trios consisted of Jay Hammel on guitar and Harold Cardwell on drums. Dave's recordings include "Anomaly," "Birthday Wish" (1994) and "Dave Hepler 4" (2001), featuring Matt Thompson on bass.

FREDDIE HUBBARD

Indianapolis-born Freddie Hubbard enjoyed his first professional engagement with two of Indiana's top jazz icons, Wes and Monk Montgomery. After moving to New York in the late 1950s, he performed with saxophonist Sonny Rollins, Slide Hampton, J.J. Johnson and Quincy Jones. In 1961, Hubbard played a long stint with the Art Blakey's Jazz Messengers. He won the *DownBeat* New Star Award for trumpet. Between 1966 and 1970, Hubbard recorded a series of his own albums on the Atlantic label. He recorded with some of the world's top jazz musicians including Oliver Nelson, Eric Dolphy, Herbie Hancock, Wayne Shorter and Max Roach. Freddie is responsible for successful recordings on Blue Note and other labels. (Photograph by Duncan Schiedt)

ALONZO "POOKIE" JOHNSON

Alonzo "Pookie" Johnson was born 1927 in Indianapolis. He attended Crispus Attucks High School and Butler University's Arthur Jordan College of Music. After leaving the U. S. Army Air Force, Johnson traveled with many bands including the Eddie Bird Sextet, Sax Kare Band, King Kolax Big Band, the Montgomery-Johnson Quintet and the Jimmy Coe Orchestra. He performed on Indiana Avenue at some of the most legendary jazz clubs including the Walker Casino, the Sunset Terrace, the British Lounge, the 440 Club, Henri's, and George's Bar. Johnson performed with Wes, Monk and Buddy Montgomery, Willis Kirk, Freddie Hubbard, Slide Hampton, Leroy Vinegar, Jimmy

ALONZO "POOKIE" JOHNSON

Coe, Russell Webster, the Hampton Sisters, and many others. His discography includes Buddy Montgomery's "Montgomery Brothers and Five Others," Russell Webster's "Together Again," Jimmy Coe's "Say What" and the compilation album "Almost Forgotten Artist's" on Columbia Records.

J. J. JOHNSON
Photograph by Duncan Schiedt

J.J. JOHNSON

J.J. Johnson was born January 22,1924 in Indianapolis. In 1942, at the age of eighteen, he joined the Benny Carter band. He later performed with the Count Basie Orchestra. In 1946, Johnson recorded in New York under his own name with the Esquire All Stars. He later performed with such name artists as Illinois Jacquet, Dizzy Gillespie, and Oscar Pittiford. In 1954, Johnson co-led a quintet with trombonist Kai Winding that toured Europe and made several memorable recordings. From 1956 through 1960, he played with his own group. In 1961, he toured with the legendary Miles Davis. As a writer, Johnson scored many compositions. In 1970, he moved to Los Angeles to pen soundtracks for movies and television. J.J. Johnson recorded, "Jay Jay Johnson All Stars" (1953), "Blue Trombone" (1959), and "A Touch Of Satin" (1962). After a short retirement in the late 1990s, Johnson passed away on Feb. 4, 2001 at the age of seventy-seven. He will be remembered as one of the world's greatest jazz trombonist. (Above photograph by Duncan Schiedt)

MINGO JONES

MINGO JONES

Mingo Jones was born December 12, 1928 in Saint Joseph, Missouri. After being stationed with the 35th U. S. Army Band at Fort Harrison, Indiana, Mingo made Indianapolis his home. In the early 1950s, Mingo had the chance to perform bass for guitarist

Photograph, left to right: Wes Montgomery – Monk Montgomery – Buddy Montgomery

Let the Good Times Roll

209

Wes Montgomery. He later became one of the top bass players of the famous Indiana Avenue scene. Jones performed with some of Indiana's top musicians such as Pookie Johnson, Jimmy Coe, Erroll Grandy, Marvin Chandler, Melvin Rhyne, David Baker, Freddie Hubbard, Slide Hampton, Everett Greene and many others. While playing a long stint at the Embers show lounge in Indianapolis, Mingo had the opportunity to back up national acts including Barbara McNair, Helen O'Connell, Bobby Short and Mel Torme. Mingo performs in the Indianapolis area continuing to play the top jazz clubs.

HARRY MIEDEMA

Saxophonist Harry Miedema began his career by playing for the Lawrence Central High School band in Indianapolis. In the early 1970s, Miedema attended Indiana University School of Music and studied under jazz icon David Baker. Miedema was music director for the O'jays for twenty-two years, and has performed with such artists Lou Rawl, Natalie Cole and the Temtations. Television performance's include The Today Show, Oprah Winfrey and the Quincy Jones show, Vibe.

BUDDY MONTGOMERY
MONK MONTGOMERY

Wes Montgomery may have garnered most of the headlines with his talents on the guitar, but brothers Monk and Buddy left their mark on the jazz landscape as well. In 1952, Monk, while performing with the Lionel Hampton band, made musical history by becoming the first jazz musician to play the Fender electric bass. He continued to perform around the world with famed musicians who enjoyed his unique style. Monk is credited with creating the Las Vegas Jazz Society. Buddy Montgomery was the music arranger for the brothers. His favored musical instrument was the piano, but in 1957, he won the DownBeat Award for "New Star of the Year" on the vibraphone. He also won the "New Jazz Arranger of the Year" Award. He and Monk organized the Mastersounds, a quartet that was quite popular. Buddy, the only surviving Montgomery brother, lives in Los Angeles and continues to record and produce. His CD, "Buddy Montgomery, Live At Maybeck Recital Hall," is considered a classic.

WES MONTGOMERY

Born in Indianapolis, Indiana on March 6, 1925, Wes was a self-taught guitarist whose original style and the use of octaves changed the form of guitar playing. After learning to play the instrument in his teenage years and playing in local clubs, Wes was discovered by Lionel Hampton. He toured with the Hampton band in 1948. In the 1950s, he returned to

Let the Good Times Roll

Indianapolis to perform in some of the top jazz clubs. In 1957 and '58 he recorded with the Mastersounds, a group formed by his brothers Monk and Buddy Montgomery. They recorded several albums. In 1959, Wes recorded with his own trio, featuring organist Melvin Rhyne. In 1960, Wes performed briefly with the John Coltrane Sextet in San Francisco, and later recorded with the Wynton Kelly Trio. In the mid-1960s, he achieved international notoriety with his instrumental pop recordings "Goin' Out Of My Head" and "California Dreaming." In 1967 he made an appearance on television with Herb Albert. Wes died of a heart attack on June 15, 1968.

MYRIAD (1976)
Left to right: Bruce Stanforth – Larry King – Terry Cook – Royce Campbell – Art Reiner

MYRIAD

ROYCE CAMPBELL
TERRY COOK
LARRY KING
ART REINER
BRUCE STANFORTH

This jazz/fusion group was formed in the mid-1970s. It was the forerunner of the band Affinity.

OLIVER NELSON JR.

Oliver Nelson Jr. was born in St. Louis, Missouri. He moved to Indianapolis in 1979. The son of famous jazz artist Oliver Nelson, he received his master's of music performance degree on flute from Butler University in Indianapolis. Nelson has performed with his father, Oliver Nelson Sr. and recorded with Benny Golson, Bob Crenshaw, David Baker and drummer Grady Tate. In 1996, his band won the WTPI Jazz Festival Competition. He continues to leads his own band and perform at some of the top jazz clubs in Indianapolis.

OLIVER NELSON JR.
Photograph by Larry Goshen

Let the Good Times Roll

JOHN VON OHLEN
Von Ohlen performed with, among others, Billy Maxted, Woody Herman and Stan Kenton.

Let the Good Times Roll

PAULA OWEN

Singer Paula Owen was born in Columbus, Ohio. She has lived in Muncie for several years. Owen performed with the Trotty Heck Quartet at Rick's Café in downtown Indianapolis for twelve years. *Jazz Times* magazine wrote of Owens; "Paula Owen is the best-kept secret in vocal jazz." Owen's recordings include "Red, Green and Blue" with vocalist Everett Green, "What Is This Magic Happening?" with Ron Enyard, and "So Nice To Be With You" featuring saxophonist Ernie Krivda.

CARL PERKINS

Pianist Carl Perkins was born in Indianapolis on August 16, 1928. Perkins toured with such artists as Big Jay McNeely and Tiny Bradshaw. In 1949, he moved to the West Coast. He played with the Oscar Moore trio from 1953 to 54, and then performed with the Max Roach-Clifford Brown quintet. In 1956, he played with bassist Curtis Counce. Perkins can be

PAULA OWEN
Photograph by Larry Goshen

heard on recordings with such artists as Chet Baker, Jim Hall and Art Pepper. His final session was in 1958. It included his 24-bar tune "Grooveyard." This recording featured saxophonist Harold Land. Carl Perkins passed away on March 17, 1958.

KING PLEASURE

Singer King Pleasure (Clarence Beeks) was born in Oakdale, Indiana on March 24, 1922. He popularized the form of vocalizing jazz solos. In 1952, Pleasure won a talent competition at Harlem's Apollo, singing "Moody's Mood For Love." He recorded on the Prestige label and released several albums. King retired and moved to California. He died on March 21, 1981. His recordings influenced such vocalese-lovers as Georgie Fame and the Manhattan Transfer.

CLIFFORD RATLIFF

Clifford Ratliff was born on June 29, 1947 in Indianapolis. He began playing trumpet professionally on Indiana Avenue at the age of sixteen. After graduating from Crispus Attucks High School, Ratliff spent four years in the U. S. Air Force touring Southeast Asia for the USO. After returning to Indiana and receiving a music major at Indiana State University, he continued to perform with some of the top musicians in the Indianapolis area. In 1995, Clifford was a permanent member and recorded with the popular Small Talk Quintet. Ratliff has become a prominent musician in the Indianapolis area. He performs regularly with the Jimmy Coe Big Band, and continues to front his own group, The Clifford Ratliff Quintet.

CLIFFORD RATLIFF

MELVIN RHYNE

Pianist/organist Melvin Rhyne was born on October 12, 1936 in Indianapolis. His father Aldrich Rhyne, a ragtime pianist, provided Melvin the opportunity to grow up in a musical environment. Rhyne attended Crispus Attucks High School in 1949. In 1950, he performed with the R&B group, The Monarchs. In 1956, Rhyne switched from the piano to the organ. He later became more prominent on the Hammond B-3. Rhyne performed in local nightclubs such as the Turf Bar, the HubBub, 19th Hole, 440 Club, the Missile Room and Cotton Club. At those clubs Rhyne performed with Leroy Vinnegar, Freddie Hubbard, Virgil Jones and drummer "Killer" Ray Appleton. In 1959, while playing with guitarist Wes Montgomery at the Indianapolis Missile Room, saxophonist Cannonball Adderley

MELVIN RHYNE (1988)
Photograph by Larry Goshen

Let the Good Times Roll

discovered the trio. They received their first recording contract with Riverside Records. They recorded four albums: "Wes Montgomery Trio" in 1959, and "Boss Guitar," "Guitar On The Go" and "Portrait Of Wes" in 1963. Melvin performed and appeared with many great artists such as B.B. King, Della Reese, The Four Tops, Roland Kirk, Jimmy Coe and many others. He performs and records in the Indianapolis area.

LEROY VINNEGAR

Leroy Vinnegar was born in Indianapolis on July 13, 1928. He is one of the world's best known jazz bassists. Vinnegar has performed with great jazz artists including Charlie Parker, Sonny Stitt, Stan Getz, Barney Kessel and drummer Shelly Manne. In the 1960s, he performed and recorded with Sonny Rollins, Gerald Wilson, the Jazz Crusaders and Kenny Dorham, just to name a few.

Photograph left to right: Benny Barth – Leroy Vinnegar
Photograph by Duncan Schiedt

BILLY WOOTEN

Indiana-born Billy Wooten has been an international performer and recording artist for many years. His main instruments are the vibraharp and marimbas. He has performed for many dignitaries such as the President of Hungary, the Latin American Ambassador, the Prime Ministers of the Baltic States, and the President of the United States. He performed on television in such shows as Party Time Royale and Blues with a Feeling. Wooten hosted the WIFE Radio show Jazz after Dark. Billy has recorded for many national labels including Chess, Atlantic, United Artists and Blue Note. In addition to his own recordings, he has performed on major labels with Richard Evans & The Soulful Strings, and guitarist Grant Green.

BILLY WOOTEN

Let the Good Times Roll

DAVID YOUNG

Indianapolis resident David Young majored in music at Kentucky State College, Butler and Indiana University. After completing military service with the Third Armored Division Band, David performed in New York with the George Russell Sextet. They recorded "Jazz in the Space Age," The George Russell Sextet at the Five Spot," Statuspunk," and "The George Russell Sextet in Kansas City." He performed and toured with the Lionel Hampton Orchestra. While with Hampton, he recorded the jazz album "The Newport Uproar." David has performed and recorded with many other major artists such as Frank Foster, Jack McDuff and The Grover Mitchell Jazz Orchestra. He recorded his own album self-titled "David Young," on the Mainstream Label. David toured with the Duke Ellington Orchestra under the direction of Mercer Ellington. He has accompanied such artists as Sarah Vaughn, Ella Fitzgerald, Joe Williams, Nancy Wilson, Tony Bennett, Della Reece, and the great Cab Calloway.

Photograph left to right: David Baker (trombone) – David Young (sax) – Larry Ridley (bass) – Wes Montgomery (guitar) (1958)
Photograph by Duncan Schiedt

Let the Good Times Roll

Photograph left to right: Michael Brown and Chatterbox proprietor David Andrichik. (On stage at the Chatterbox (1996)
Photograph by Larry Goshen

INDIANA ROOTS WITH THE STAN KENTON ORCHESTRA (1972)
1. Chuck Carter 2. Dick Schearer
3. Ramon Lopez

JAZZ NOTABLES

AL COBINE
AL KIGER
ALAN REEVE
AMY STEPHENS
ARETTA LA MARRE
BARRY KETTERY
BILL LANCTON
BILL MOSS
BILL MYERS
CARL HINES
CAROLL DE CAMP
CATHY MORRIS
CHARLIE SMITH
CHRIS PYLE
CHUCK CARTER
CLAUDE SIFFERLEN
CLAUDE THORNHILL
DAN SMITH
DAVE ATKINS
DICK LASWELL
DICK REEVES
DON WILHITE
DONNA LIVELY CLARK
EARL COE
EVERETT GREENE
FRANK SMITH
FRANK STEANS
FRED MONROE
FRED WITHROW
GARY WALTERS
GENE MARKIEWICZ

GEORGE MACK
GREGG BACON
HAL SMITH
HANS STURM
HAROLD CARDWELL
JACK HELSLEY
JACK PHELAN
JAMES BELL
JAMES SPAULDING
JAN ALDRIDGE CLARK
JANIECE JAFFE
JEFF DEHERDT
JERRY COKER
JIM ALBRECHT
JIM EDISON
JIM FARRELLY
JIMMY MUMFORD
JOE DEAL
JOHN HILL
JOHN HUBER
JOHN SPICKNALL
JOHN VON OHLEN
JONATHAN WOOD
JOZELL CARTER
JULIE SPENCER
KEN GOTSCHALL
KENI WASHINGTON
KENNY KIPP
KENNY PHELPS
KEVIN ANKER
KEVIN JOHNSON

Let the Good Times Roll

KEVIN KAISER
KYLE QUASS
LANCASTER PRICE
LARRY CALLAND
LARRY LIGGETT
LARRY RIDLEY
LARRY WISEMAN
MALCOLM LEWIS
MARK BUSELLI
MARK CRAVENS
MARVIN CHANDLER
MARY ANN MOSS
MICHAEL BROWN
MICHAEL STRICKLIN
MIKE CUNNINGHAM
MONIKA HERZIG
OLIVER EUBANKS
OLIVER NELSON JR
PAUL PARKER
PAUL PLUMMER
PAUL SMOKER
PAUL SUROWIAK
PEGGY SHELDON
PETE DAILY
PETE WILHOIT
PETER KIENLE
PHAREZ WHITTED
RAY APPLETON
REGINALD DU VALLE
ROB DIXON
ROBERT COLEMAN
RON BRINSON
RON ENYARD
RON MILES
RUSSELL WEBSTER
RUSTY HUMPHREY
SAM GIBSON
SARA CASWELL
SCOTT STROMAN
SCOTT VALLATINE
STAN HILL
STEVE BALL
STEVE DOKKEN
STEVE ROBINETTE
STEVE WOERNER
STEVE WEAKLEY
TERRY COOK
THREE-WAY STREET
TIM BRICKLEY
TOM CLARK
TOM MULLINIX
TONY MEDEIROS
TROTTY HECK
VICKIE DANIELS
VIRGIL JONES
VIRGINIA JEFFERSON
WILLIAM "WHITEY" HARRIS
WILLIAM BOKYD

WILLIE BAKER
WILLIS KIRK
WINTON REYNOLDS

Let the Good Times Roll

Miscellaneous

THE HAMILTON MOVEMENT

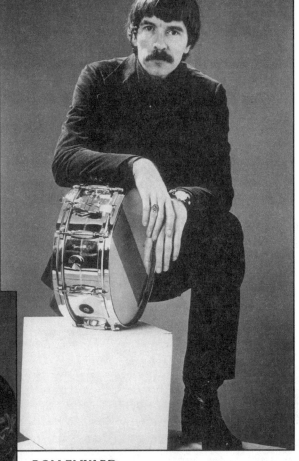

RON ENYARD

PURE GOLD

LIGHT 3D

DAVE MORGAN TRIO

TOGETHERNESS IS'

AL WALTON TRIO
With JOY SMITH

WE-3

YOUNG SET

THE KELLY JAY ORCHESTRA

TOMMY BRANHAM

FAIR WARNING

Let the Good Times Roll

PHOTOGRAPH CREDITS

Art Adams, Art Adams collection - Amos Arthur, Arthur's Music Store – "Bouncin' Bill" Baker, Bill Baker collection — Boyd Bennett, Boyd Bennett collection – The Blue Angels, Lillian Boles –The Boppers, Jimmy Guilford – Jimmy Clendening, Don Holt – Jimmy Coe Orchestra, Jimmy Coe – The Contemporaries, Gerald Ruark - The Counts, Dave Williams – The Crowns, L. Goshen – The Deb Tones, Jimmy Mack – Danny Dollar, Morgan Schumacher collection – Downbeats, Morgan Schumacher collection - Chuck Berry & Morgan Schumacher, L. Goshen – Jackie De Shannon, L. Goshen - The Fascinators, Don Kelley – The Five Stars, Jim Bruhn – The Four Freshmen, Duncan Schiedt - The Four Sounds, Jimmy Guilford – Jimmy Ganzberg & Jimmy Mack, L. Goshen – Jimmy Ganzberg, J. Ganzberg – 1958 Jimmy Coe Group, Jerry Williams Collection – Larry Gardner, L. Gardner – Gary Gillespie, Don Kelley col. – Hampton Sisters, Virtue Hampton – Duke Hampton Band, Virtue Hampton – Ronnie Haig, L. Goshen – Bobby Helms, Jerry Williams Col. – Johnny & The Pyramids, Dan Beach – Keetie & The Kats, Don Holt & Loughery's Studio – Larry Lee & Keith Phillips, L. Gardner - The Labels, Don Kelley – Bobby Lewis, Bobby Lewis col. – Jimmy Mack, J. Mack Col. – Lonnie Mack, L. Mack – Jack Morrow, Loughery's Studio –Nooney Rickett, Don Kelley – Rooker & The Rockers, Don Holt – Jerry Seifert, Don Kelley – The Showman, Doug Sterns – The Crowns Live, L Goshen – Larry Goshen, Herb Goshen – Jerry Lee Williams & The Crowns, L. Goshen – Tommy Wills, Tommy Wills - Dale Wright, D. Wright & Dr. Pepper – Al Young, Al Young – Jimi Hendrixf & Al Young, Al Young - Boys Next Door, Don Holt – The Checkmates,Ltd., Sonny Charles – The Chosen Few, Carl Storie – Coven, Steve Ross – The Dawn Five, Don Holt – The Heavy, Phil Thompson – The Highlighters, Jason Yoder - The Idle Few, Ron Benneth – Jackson Five, Don Kelley collection - Joys Of Life, Jim Albrecht – The Knightsmen, Karl Hinkle – The McCoys, Bob Berry – Keith Murphy & Daze, Keith Murphy - Reb Porter, Jimmy Mack – The Rivieras, Miriam Linna – The Sentimentals, B & L Photographers - The Shy Ones, Bonnie McDowell – Sounds Unlimited, Wayne Wilson – The Torkays, Keith Murphy - The Accents, Vince Sanders – Andy Anderson & The Jets, J. Ganzberg - Marden Baker Quintet, L. Goshen – The Blue Tones, Cale & Whyte – By/Counts, M. James – The Cavaliers, L. Goshen – Ray Churchman, Louis J. McMahon & Melvin James Col. – The Classmen, M. James – The Crackerjack, L. Goshen – Bobby Dark & Darlene Dowler, D. Dowler – The Dawnbeats #2, L. Gardner – Del & The Roadrunners, D. Bailey – Bill Stewart, Delbert Bailey & Charlie Rich, D. Bailey – The Pacesetters, D. Demaree – Danny Dollar & The Coins, L. Goshen – The Dukes, Jim Hickman – The Epics, P. Hutchinson – The Epics, Art Adams – The Five Checks, Cale & Whyte – The Five Cords, D. Kelley – The First Impression, Louis J. McMahon & Melvin James col. – Flo Garvin, F. Garvin – Suzanne Prince Band, Gilbert Gordon - Jimmy Guilford, J. Guilford – The Inner Circle, Guy Tarrents – Jess & The Jokers, J. Colburn – The Jewels, G. LeMaster – Sons Of The Pioneers, G. LeMaster – Jimmy & The Exceptions, G. Tarrents – Orly Knutson Trio, J. Ganzberg – Tommy Lam, Jerry Williams Col. – Jimmy McDaniels & Pete Funk, L. Goshen – The Monograms, Bob Bernard

Let the Good Times Roll

– Mary Moss & King & Mary, Mary Moss - The Original Dukes, Jim Hickman
– The Keith Phillips VI, K. Phillips – Salt & Pepper, Dan Hailey – Screaming
Jimmy, D. Bailey – The Sportsmen, Irv Levy – The Swingin' Lads, Don Kelley
– Teach & The Tracers, Larry Gardner – The Travells, J. Jacobsen – Tuttle &
The Shells, J. Ganzberg – Eddie Walker & The Demons, Larry Gardner – Step
Wharton, Billboard – Dean Wolfe, L. Goshen – The American Cast, Scott
McDowell Amnesty, Louis J. McMahon & Melvin Walden Col. – Black Magic,
Allen Burke - Darlene Dowler, D. Dowler – The Chain Reaction, D. Dowler
– The Faith Band, Carl Storie – The Fifth Admendment, L. Goshen – Fingers,
Allen Burke - Five Easy Pieces, Jimmy Mack – Fresh, Bill Lancton – Jim Gerrard
& Jack Gilfoy, J. Gilfoy – Jimmy Guilford Band, J. Guilford – John Hiatt, Vector
Management – Michael Jackson, Don Kelley Col. - Jubal Band, Howard Phillips
– Brad Long, B. Long – Madison Zane, Louis J. McMahon & Melvin Walden Col.
– Manchild, Louis J. McMahon & Melvin Walden Col. – John Mellencamp, Don
Kelley col. – Rapture, Rodney Stepp - Rich Kids, Rick Childress – Roadmaster,
Mercury Records – Them Changes, L. Goshen – Duke Tumatoe,
Gary Brewer – Wright Brothers, T. Wright – Zerfas, Howard Phillips – Acid
Green, Gregg Stewart – Deliverance, Jimmy Mack Photo's – Darren Dowler, D.
Dowler – The Tyme, D. Dowler – The Lettermen, D. Dowler – The Equalizers,
Jinx Dawson – The First Impression, Jimmy Mack – The Girls, Julie Gerard
– Group Theropy, Jimmy Mack - Barbara Higbie, Irene Young – Illicit Affair,
Rick Childress – Janet Jackson, Don Kelley col. - La Toya Jackson, RCA
Records – Jubal Band, Howard Phillips – Light, Jimmy Mack – Malachi,
Louis J. McMahon & Melvin Walden col. – Motley Crue, Don Kelley Col. -
Mathematicians, Kevin Kouts – Carrie Newcomer, Senor McGuire – P. S. Dump
Your Boyfriend, Gary James Prod. – Red Beans & Rice, Yun Hui – John "BJ"
Rogers, B. Rogers – R.S.V.P., Delbert Bailey – The Starlettes, Gary James Prod.
– Carl Storie, C. Storie – Mark Collie, John Casella, Bill Brunt, Carl Storie, C.
Storie collection – Henry Lee Summer, Gary James Prod. – Sweetwater, L.
Goshen – Why On Earth, Yun Hui - Wildfire, J. Jacobsen – Cathy Morris & Mike
Berry, L. Goshen – Blaq Lily, Blaq Lily – Phil T. Blues, Phil Thompson – Tim
Brickley, Brickley – Buzzy Jones, Louis McCahon & Melvin James col. – Larry
Calland, Calland – Jan Aldridge Clark, L. Goshen – Governor Davis, Yun
Hui – Kara Day, L. Goshen – Gene Deer, L. Goshen – Jennie Devoe, L. Goshen
– Dog Talk, Yun Hui – Steve Dokken, L. Goshen – Drama Queen, Julie Gerard
– Leta Essig, L. Goshen – Ronnie Haig Band, L. Goshen – Pletchers & Haig, L.
Goshen – Monika Herzig, L. Goshen – Peter Kienle, L. Goshen – Kevin Johnson,
L. Goshen – Cynthia Layne, L. Goshen – Ann McWilliams, L. Goshen – Cathy
Morris, L. Goshen – Plaid Descent, Ann McWilliams – Jess Richmond, Yun Hui
– Roadhouse, L. Goshen – Rozen Bombs, Yun Hui – Small Talk, Jim Albrecht
– Charlie Smith, CS Productions – Frank Steans, L. Goshen – Rodney Stepp, R.
Stepp – Darren Stroud, L. Goshen – Trinia Cox, Ken Pace – The Gypsies, Jim
Albrecht – Yun Hui, L. Goshen – Jerry Williams & Chenowith, J. Williams – Kim
Cronley, Cronley – Jan Edwards & Joe Edwards, J. Edwards – Day, Flint, Skinner
& Gibson, T. Flint - Janie Frickie, McGuire &Columbia Records – Crystal Gayle,
Gayle fan club – Lattie Moore, L. Moore – Ragsdale, Highland, Moore, Chickie
Rindles, Phillips & Blair, L. Moore – The Haymakes, Jack Morrow – Chickie &
Morrow, J. Morrow – Lenny Ray, J. Williams – Running On Empty, J. Jacobsen

Let The Good Times Roll

Order Information

To order copies of *Let The Good Times Roll, An Anthology of Indiana Music,* please:

Telephone the publisher, Books For Life Foundation, at
317-685-2500, or Six Dogs Gifts and Books at 317-916-1305

Write to *Let The Good Times Roll* at Books For Life Foundation at
1060 Virginia Avenue, Indianapolis, Indiana 46203

Email through the Books For Life Foundation Web Site at
www.booksforlifefoundation.com

Visit Six Dogs Gifts and Books at 1060 Virginia Avenue,
Historic Fountain Square, Indianapolis, Indiana.

Books For Life Foundation is a not-for-profit organization
dedicated to educating aspiring authors regarding the publishing
process. More information about the foundation and how you can
help new literary voices be heard can be learned by contacting
Mark Shaw, Amy Lain, or Bis Whitacre on the Internet at
www.booksforlifefoundation.com or by telephoning 317-685-2500.

List Of Indiana Notables

AARON BURNELL
AARON DISTLER
AARON VAUGHN-STROOP
ACID GREEN
ADA STRAUB
ADAM SMASHER
AFTER 7
AL (ALPHONSO) YOUNG
AL COBINE
AL FICKLIN
AL NOYD
AL OFFERCER
AL WALTON TRIO
AL YATES
ALAN JONES
ALBATROSS
ALETRA HAMPTON
ALEX PARKEVICH
ALLEN "TURK" BURKE
ALLEN KIRSCH
ALLEN ROTH
ALLIGATOR BROS.
ALLISON & CALVIN TURNER
ALLISON TURNER
ALONZO "POOKIE" JOHNSON
AMNESTY
AMOS ARTHUR
AMY PENROD
AMY STEPHENS
ANDERSON WHITE
ANDRA FAYE
ANDRE'
ANDREW FISH
ANDROPOV'S ASSASINS
ANDY ANDERSON
ANDY REYIA
ANDY RICHARDS
ANGIE WALKER
ANN MC WILLIAMS
ANN WAGNER
ANTHONY COOPER
APRIL HALBROOK
ARLEY PRICE
ART ADAMS
ART REINER
ASHER BEN RUBY
ASTRONAUTS
AUBREY CAGLE
AVANTI
AVIE CALENDER
AXAS
AZTEX
BABYFACE
BACK STREET
BANDIT

BARB GABRIEL
BARBARA HIGBIE
BARRY KEM
BARRY KETTERY
BASOOTIES
BEA ISAACS
BEAU BRINKLEY
BEAUTIFUL AUTHENTIC-ZOO
GODS
BECKI HOLLAND
BEEBLE BROX
BEN HICKMAN
BENNY BARTH
BIG DADDY GRAHAM
BIG MOE
BIG MOE & THE PANICS
BIGGER THAN ELVIS
BILL BAKER
BILL BOGBY
BILL BROOKS
BILL CAMPBELL
BILL COOPER
BILL DICKIE
BILL ELLIS
BILL EVANS
BILL FLIEHMAN
BILL HARRIS
BILL KIRKPATRICK
BILL KNIPE
BILL LANCTON
BILL LEVIN
BILL LYNCH
BILL MOSLEY
BILL MYERS
BILL RILEY
BILL RITTER
BILL ROBERTS
BILL ROOKER
BILL SETTLES
BILL SHEARER
BILL SHERRIL
BILL STEWART
BILL VALE
BILL WEDSNER
BILL WHARTON
BILL WILSON
BILL WITHERSPOON
BILLY BALL & UPSETTERS
BILLY DAY
BILLY LOVE
BILLY MERCURY
BILLY MOORE
BILLY NIGHTSHADE
BILLY RICE
BILLY WARREN

BILLY WOOTEN
BILLY YOUNG
BIRDMEN OF ALCATRAZ
BITTERSWEET-BRIDGE
BLACK & BLUE
BLACK MAGIC
BLACK MARKET
BLACKSTONE
BLAKE BABIES
BLAQ LILY
BLIND OTIS
BLITZ KIDS
BLUE COLLAR
BLUE HUGH & COLOR
BLUE PRINT
BLUES INC.
BO WALLACE
BOB & TOM
BOB (CHICO) PENICK
BOB BERNARD
BOB BOGEL
BOB BRIETUNG
BOB BROWN
BOB CARRIE
BOB CEIPE
BOB CRABTREE
BOB DAWSON
BOB DEAL (MICK MARS)
BOB EDWARDS
BOB FIELDS
BOB FLANIGAN
BOB FOLGER
BOB JONES
BOB LANNARD
BOB LUCAS
BOB MIX
BOB SCHUSTER
BOB SNYDER
BOB THOMPSON
BOB WILSON
BOBBIE PETERSON
BOBBY DARK
BOBBY HELMS
BOBBY JOHNS
BOBBY LEE
BOBBY LEWIS
BOBBY PHILLIPS
BOBBY RIDENOUR
BOBBY STREHL
BOBBY TOON
BODACIOUS
BONNIE MC DOWELL
BOYD (POPCORN) JOHNSON
BOYD BENNETT
BRAD ESTES

Let the Good Times Roll

BRAD GARTON
BRAD LONG
BRAIN SISTER
BRAMBLE GRIT
BRANDON GIBSON
BRETT DONOVAN
BRIAN CHRISTOPHER
BRIAN DE WITT
BRIAN E. PAULSON
BRIAN WOOLRIDGE
BRIAR ROSE
BRIDGEWATER
BRUCE "SNOOKY" COONS
BRUCE ANDERSON
BRUCE COOMBS
BRUCE HAINEY
BRUCE STANFORTH
BRUCE STUCKLEY
BRUCE WATERMAN
BRYAN DISBRO
BRYAN HIGHTOWER
BRYAN ZERFAS
BUD OSBORNE
BUDDY VAN OSDOL
BUTCH SANDLIN
BUZZY JONES
BY/COUNTS
BYRON SMALL
CAL COLLINS
CALVIN SHIELDS
CALVIN TURNER
CAPTAIN STEELE
CARL HINES
CARL JUNIOR CAMPBELL
CARL LoSASSO
CARL PERKINS
CARL RAINGE
CARL STORIE
CARMALITA HAMPTON
CAROL BUCKOSKI
CARRIE NEWCOMER
CARROLL DE CAMP
CAT SADLER
CATHY MORRIS
CELEBRATE
CHAMPION BAND
CHANCES 'R
CHARENCE DORSEY
CHARLES ANDERSON
CHARLES BIDWELL
CHARLES COTTON
CHARLES TURNER
CHARLEY HINKLE
CHARLIE (BROWN) CLARK
CHARLIE ANDERSON
CHARLIE KENDAL
CHARLIE SMITH
CHARLIE STEWART

CHERRY LYNN
CHERRYL HAYES
CHERYL GURNELL-PIERSON
CHESTER BROWN
CHET SAWYER
CHICK HOPKINS
CHICK MC HENRY
CHOOCH & ENCHANTERS
CHRIS ALLEN
CHRIS BROWNING
CHRIS CLARK
CHRIS DICKINSON
CHRIS LIEBER
CHRIS NEILSEN
CHRIS PYLE
CHRIS SHAFFER
CHRIS SKILLMAN
CHUCK BAKER
CHUCK BEST
CHUCK BUSH
CHUCK CARTER
CHUCK CUNNINGHAM
CHUCK DEAN
CHUCK ELLIS
CHUCK HIGGINS
CHUCK WALLACE
CHURCHYARD
CINDERS
CIRCLES
CLAUDE SIFFERLEN
CLAYTONS
CLIFF FORTNEY
CLIFF WHITE
CLIFFORD RATLIFF
CLOSE QUARTERS
CLYDE EARL
CODA
CONGA JAZZ
CONNIE SMITH
CORKY KIRK
CORKY WHITEMAN
CORVETTES
COUNT FISHER
COUNTRY BOB
COUNTRY COUSIN-CHICKIE
COUSINS FROM VENUS
COZY JOHNSON
CRAIG BLATTNER
CRAIG GARDENER
CRAIG HAMILTON
CRAIG TERRY
CREATIONS
CREPE SOUL
CROCKETT & COMPANY
CRUISE CONTROL
CRUISEMATICS
CRYSTAL GAYLE
CRYSTAL TALIEFERO

CURLY MYERS
CURT ROBINETTE
CYN HAMMOND
CYNTHIA LAYNE
CZM
D. C. MULLINS
D. L. BYRON
DADDY JACK DICE
DAL BAKER
DALE KRANTZ
DALE LAWRENCE
DALE SOPHIEA
DALE SPURLOCK
DALE WRIGHT
DALLAS MILLER
DAMASCUS ROAD
DAN BOTNICH
DAN HAILEY
DAN HALL
DAN HANLEY
DAN MC LEAN
DAN METRO
DAN VONNEGUT
DANDELION WINE
DANE CLARK
DANNY (DOWLER) DOLLAR
DANNY BEACH
DANNY BROWN
DANNY DAIN
DANNY DOLLAR & THE COINS
DANNY MC MULLIN
DANNY ORNUNG
DANNY SMITH
DANNY STAFFORD
DARLENE (DOWLER) DOLLAR
DARREL CHENOWITH
DARRELL BALL
DARREN DOWLER
DARREN STROUD
DARYL SIMMONS
DAVE BARNES
DAVE BEHNKE
DAVE BENNETT
DAVE BURRIS
DAVE DERRIKSON
DAVE DUNNE
DAVE ELLMAN
DAVE ELMORE
DAVE FLANNERY
DAVE GEISLER
DAVE GOLDMAN
DAVE GRISSOM
DAVE HALL
DAVE HEPLER
DAVE HOLCOMB
DAVE HOOPER
DAVE HUFFMAN
DAVE JONES

Let the Good Times Roll

DAVE KELLIE	DICK WALTERS	EDDY & SOUL BAND
DAVE MARTIN	DICK YORK	EDDY CONRAD
DAVE MC KOWN	DICKENS	EDDY HUMPHREY
DAVE MERRIS	DINO CODALATA	EDGAR BATEMAN
DAVE MORGAN	DIREWOLF	ELDRIDGE MORRISON
DAVE PLEISS	DOBY LONDON	ELEANOR LEE
DAVE POST	DOCTOR SEUSS	ELFIN HILL
DAVE RANDLE	DOG TALK	ELLIOTT JACKSON
DAVE THOMPSON	DON BARBOUR	ELLMAN-JAMES DUO
DAVE TRUEBLOOD	DON BASORE	EMERGENCY EXIT
DAVE WASHBURN	DON DAVIDSON	EMILY BONUS
DAVE WEBSTER	DON ELLIS	EMILY JACKSON
DAVE WILKERSON	DON EWIGLIBEN	EMMANUEL OFFICER
DAVE WORKMAN	DON HERALD	ERC JOHNSON
DAVE ZERFAS	DON HIGGS	ERIC BEAADE
DAVID ALLEE	DON KELLEY	ERIC BLATTNER
DAVID BAKER	DON MAIN	ERIC BROWN
DAVID DARLING	DON RAMSEY	ERIC GRIMMET
DAVID LARMAN	DON WILHITE	ERIC WHITE
DAVID LEE	DONALD LEE	ERNEST GRIFFIN
DAVID LEE ROTH	DONALD MC PHERSON	ERNEST WARREN
DAVID LERCHEY	DONALD PORTER	ERROLL GRANDY
DAVID MILLER	DONNA LIVELY CLARK	ESQUIRES
DAVID MORGAN	DONNY SANDERS	EUGENE FOWLKES
DAVID WAIT	DOUG ADAMS	EUGENE SMITH
DAVID YOUNG	DOUG CAIN	EVA JO
DAWN HAMPTON	DOUG DENTON	EVE RENE'
DAZE	DOUG GEAN	EVERETT GREENE
DEAN CHILDRESS	DOUG HILL	EZRA TODD SHELTON
DEAN TAGGART	DOUG MC COY	FABULOUS JOKERS
DEAN WAGNER	DOUG METCIK	FAITH BAND
DEAN WOLFE	DOUG STAUCH	FALKANS
DEB MULLINS	DOUG STERNS	FAST FORWARD
DEBRA LOUISE	DOW JONES & THE	FAT BOY
DECEMBER'S-CHILDREN	INDUSTRIALS	FEEBEE & THE RAGWEED PATCH
DEEP WATER	DR. VIRGINIA-JEFFERSON	FESTIVAL
DEFIANCE	DRAMA QUEEN	FINGERS
DEL & THE ROADRUNNERS	DREAM FEVER	FIVE EASY PIECES
DELBERT BAILEY	DUANE "BUSSARD" GARVIN	FLAME
DELIVERANCE	DUANE BURKE	FLO GARVIN
DENIE SMERDEL	DUANE ROLAND	FOUR OF A KIND
DENIECE WILLIAMS	DUKE DEMAREE	FOURTH ROOM
DENNIS ALEXANDER	DUKE HAMPTON	FRANCIS "SCRAPPER"
DENNIS LEAS	DUKE TUMATOE	BLACKWELL
DENNIS TURNER	DWAYNE KENDALL	FRANK AGUILAR
DENNY WILSON	DWIGHT HOWARD	FRANK DEAN
DENVER LEE	EARL "FOX" WALKER	FRANK GLOVER
DIANE FERGUSON	EBONY RHYTHM	FRANK PUZZULLO
DICK DEWAYNE	ECLIPSE	FRANK SMITH
DICK DICKINSON	ED BURNS	FRANK STEANS
DICK DONAHUE	ED COX	FRANK WECHSLER
DICK GENTILE	ED JARMAN	FRANKIE WATTERS
DICK GREEN	ED PITTMAN	FRED HOSTETTER
DICK LASWELL	EDDIE (LITTLE-EIDDIE) JEFFERS	FRED LAWSON
DICK NEAT	EDDIE CONDON	FRED MONROE
DICK PETTENGER	EDDIE GREEN	FRED WILLIAMS
DICK REEVES	EDDIE WALKER	FRED WITHROW
DICK SUMMERS	EDDIE WIEL	FREDA LOVE

Let the Good Times Roll

FREDDIE HUBBARD
FREDDY & THE-
FRESH
FRUIT LOOPS
FRUMAN BROWN
FUNDER COOPER
FUNK INC
G. C. EGY
G. DON TRUBOY
GALABOOCHES
GARY "RILEY" ANDERSON
GARY BEDELL
GARY BREWER
GARY CHECKEYE
GARY COAN
GARY DRAPER
GARY GILLESPIE
GARY HAMILTON
GARY JACOBSEN
GARY JONES
GARY KELLETT
GARY LE MASTER
GARY MC CARTY
GARY MC KIERNAN
GARY THAXTON
GARY WALTERS
GARY WASSON
GENE DEER
GENE JINKS
GENE JONES
GENE LYNN
GENE MARKIEWICZ
GENE ROBINSON
GENE WHEELER
GENE WHITTHERHOLT
GEORGE ABELL
GEORGE BLACK
GEORGE CARTER
GEORGE HILES
GERALD GREGORY
GERALD RUARK
GERALDINE HAAS
GILBERT GORDON
GLEN DOUGLAS
GLEN SHERMAN
GLEN WESTERFIELD
GLENN PHARRIS
GOOD SEED
GORDON BONHAM
GOST RIDERS
GOVERNOR DAVIS
GREG ANDERSON
GREG BEALL
GREG FUNK
GREG GALBRAITH
GREG HEDGES
GREG HORN
GREG JOHNSON

GREG NICOLOFF
GREG OSBORNE
GREG STEWART
GREG STORT
GREGG BACON
GROUP THEROPY
GRY IRWIN
GUNS N' ROSES
GUS TEPEE
GUY TARRENTS
GYM STOFFER
HAJI BABA
HAL KATZCH
HARLEY KLOPFENSTEIN
HAROLD CARDWELL
HAROLD ELERY
HAROLD KNIGHT
HARRISON TURNER
HARRY CANGANY
HARRY MAGINITY
HARVEY COOK
HARVEY GROVE
HARVEY TREES
HARY MIEDEMA
HEATHER CRAIG
HEIRBORNE
HELEN SPARKS
HENRY LEE SUMMER
HERB PERKINS
HERB PROCTOR
HERBIE CRAWFORD
HERD
HERMAN LEWIS
HICKORY WIND
HIGH GROUND
HIGHLIGHTERS
HILLARD DUERSON
HILLBILLY DELUXE
HILTON HUDSON
HIM HER & THEM
HITCHCOCK- RAILROAD
HOAGY CARMICHAEL
HOOK, LINE & SINKER
HOWARD O'BROOK
HOWARD PHILLIPS
HOWIE NICHOLS
HUGO SMOOTH
ICE AGE
ILLICIT AFFAIR
INDIANA JONES
INNER CIRCLE
J. HUFFAKER
J. J. JOHNSON
J. KOSS
J.J. PEARSON
JACK ALDRICH
JACK CHILDS
JACK EADON

JACK GILFOY
JACK GLOVER
JACK HAMILTON
JACK HELSLEY
JACK LEWIS
JACK MORROW
JACK SCOTT
JACK SIMPSON
JACK WAGLEY
JACKIE ASHER
JACKIE BLAIR
JACKIE DE SHANNON
JACKIE DEE
JACKIE JACKSON
JACKSON WADE
JACLYN ODDI
JADES
JAKE SMITH
JAMES (SCREAMING)
CHURCHWELL
JAMES "POOKIE" HUDSON
JAMES "YANK" RACHELL
JAMES BELL
JAMES COCHRAN
JAMES DIXON
JAMES FOUNTAIN
JAMES HILL
JAMES LEE
JAMEY REID
JAN ALDRIDGE
JAN EDWARDS
JAN SANDERS
JANAS HOYT
JANIE FRICKIE
JANIECE JAFFE
JANN BROWNE
JASON BARTH
JASON BECKET
JASON BROWN
JASON ROLLER
JASON STONEWALL
JAY DAVIS
JAY HAMMEL
JAY PURVIS
JEAN CASE
JEANNE SCHULLER
JEANNIE McGILL
JEFF DOWNEY
JEFF GARDNER
JEFF GILL
JEFF HAND
JEFF HOLT
JEFF HORNBECK
JEFF ISBELL (IZZY STRIDLIN)
JEFF KETRON
JEFF LANTZ
JEFF MARTIN
JEFF MC DONALD

JEFF MC MULLIN	JIM SLACK	JOHN KELMEN
JEFF MILLS	JIM SONDAY	JOHN MC DOWELL III
JEFF PERRONE	JIM SPILKER	JOHN MILLER
JEFF PLUMMER	JIM TAYLOR	JOHN MOORE
JEFF REED	JIM TE RONDE	JOHN O'BANION
JEFF ROY	JIM THEROS	JOHN SCOTT
JEFF WILLIAMS	JIM TITTLE	JOHN SHAVER
JEFFREY STUART	JIM TUTTEROW	JOHN SMITH
JENNIE DE VOE	JIMMY & THE EXCEPTIONS	JOHN SMOTHERMAN
JENNIE MC GILL	JIMMY (SKEETER) POWERS	JOHN TABOR
JENNIFER AYERS	JIMMY ANDERSON	JOHN TALBOT
JENNIFER KIRK	JIMMY BRUHN	JOHN VARDIMAN
JENNIFER SPARKS	JIMMY CHENOWITH	JOHN VON OHLEN
JENNY DAVIS	JIMMY CLENDENING	JOHN ZEPS
JENNY SWEANY	JIMMY COE	JOHNNY & THE PYRAMIDS
JERICHO	JIMMY ELLIOTT	JOHNNY ATKINS
JERMAINE JACKSON	JIMMY GANZBERG	JOHNNY BENNETT
JEROME MILLS	JIMMY GUILFORD	JOHNNY CARSON
JERRY ASHER	JIMMY MACK	JOHNNY HIGHLAND
JERRY COLLINS	JIMMY MC DANIELS	JOHNNY HILAND
JERRY JAQUESS	JIMMY SCRUGGS	JOHNNY MEDVESCEK
JERRY LEE WILLIAMS	JINX DAWSON	JOHNNY MOORE
JERRY ROBERTSON	JO ANN WILSON	JOHNNY QUEST
JERRY SEIFERT	JOAN E. HALL	JOHNNY RAY
JERRY TERRIS	JOE BISHOP	JOHNNY SOCKO
JERRY THOMPSON	JOE DAVIS	JOHNNY VULCAN
JERRY WOODWARD	JOE DEAL	JON MARTIN
JES RICHMOND	JOE EDWARDS	JON SLAUGHTER
JESS & THE JOKERS	JOE HINTON	JONATHON WOODS
JESS COLBURN	JOE JACKSON	JONNY QUEST
JETTA CRUSE	JOE JOE WEEKEND	JOSE C. JOVEN
JIM & DAN BOWLIN	JOE PENNELL	JOSH GIBSON
JIM "DANDY" FIELDS	JOE RUDD	JOY SMITH
JIM ADAMS	JOE SCHREINER	JOYCE & THE COLONELS
JIM AGUILAR	JOE STANLEY	JOYCE DAVIS
JIM ALBRECHT	JOE STOUT	JOYCE DE FORD
JIM BENGE	JOE TIPPE	JOYS OF LIFE
JIM BOWERS	JOE UTTER	JOZELL CARTER
JIM CALVIN	JOEY MEANS	JUBAL BAND
JIM CARSEY	JOHN (COUGAR)	JULIE GERARD
JIM CHENOWITH	MELLENCAMP	JULIE MITCHELL
JIM CRAWFORD	JOHN (REIDER) HENRY	JULIE SPENCER
JIM CROSSEN	JOHN "BJ" ROGERS	JULIE WILSON
JIM EDISON	JOHN ASHER	KAMBRAST JAMN
JIM EDWARDS	JOHN BARGE	KAPRIS
JIM FARRELLY	JOHN BIGGS	KARA DAY
JIM FOLEY	JOHN BUNCH	KAREN LEMASTERS
JIM GARDNER	JOHN BYRNE	KARL HINKLE
JIM GAUMER	JOHN CASCELLA	KATALINAS
JIM HEPLER	JOHN DINWIDDIE	KATHY STRAKIS
JIM HICKMAN	JOHN ENGELLAND	KEETIE & THE KASUALS
JIM JACKSON	JOHN HADDIX	KEITH (KEETIE)-PHILLIPS
JIM KENNEDY & SATANS	JOHN HARDING	KEITH DOLLINS
JIM KOSS	JOHN HENRY	KEITH KILMER
JIM LITCHFIELD	JOHN HIATT	KEITH MITCHELL
JIM RYSER	JOHN HILL	KEITH MURPHY
JIM SHELTON	JOHN HOBBS	KEITH O'CONNER
JIM SHINDELL	JOHN HURST	KEITH PHELPS

Let the Good Times Roll

KEITH PHILLIPS VI
KELLEY MILLIGAN
KELLY JAY ORCH.
KELLY OLIVER
KEN GOTSCHALL
KEN MAHLKE
KEN SCHEIDLER
KENNETH SMITH
KENNY ARONOFF
KENNY EDMONDS
KENNY KIPP
KENNY LEE & THE ROYALS
KENNY LEE-KERNODLE
KENNY MOORE
KENNY NEAL
KENNY PHELPS
KENNY REYNOLDS
KENNY SHULL
KENNY TIBBETS
KENNY WASHINGTON
KENT WEINEKE
KETCH
KEVIN "FLASH" FERRELL
KEVIN ANKER
KEVIN BAXTER
KEVIN BEAN
KEVIN EDMONDS
KEVIN JOHNSON
KEVIN KAISER
KEVIN KOUTS
KEVIN McBRIDE
KEVIN RESNOVER
KEVIN SILVA
KEVIN TEAR
KHAZAD DOOM
KILLER RAY-APPLETON
KILO
KIM & MAURICE
KIM CRONLEY
KIM SCHILLING
KIMMER SMITH
KING PLEASURE
KING'S MEN
KURTIS HIGGINS
KY CURLY
KYLE QUASS
L.V. HAMMOND
LA TOYA JACKSON
LA-FENDERS
LARRY ABRAMS
LARRY ALLEN
LARRY ANDERSON
LARRY BURCH
LARRY CALLAND
LARRY CRANE
LARRY DEAL
LARRY FISSEL
LARRY FUQUA

LARRY GARDNER
LARRY GINDHART
LARRY GOSHEN
LARRY HUFFMAN
LARRY INGLE
LARRY KING
LARRY LEE
LARRY MC CULLOUGH
LARRY NOLAN (BIG TWIST)
LARRY PARISH
LARRY SAUER
LARRY SCOTT
LARRY SMEYAK
LARRY STREUBER
LARRY WHITTEN
LATE SHOW
LATEX NOVELTIES
LATTIE MOORE
LAWRENCE CLARK III
LEE JAY McCULLOUGH
LEE MORRELL
LEMON PIPERS
LENNON BROTHERS
LENNY RAY
LENNY WILSON
LEO CORNETT
LEO KEMPF
LEROY MASSEY
LEROY VINNEGAR
LESTER WILLIAMS
LETA ESSIG
LEWIS S. JONES
LIGHT
LIGHT 3D
LIMOUSINE
LINDA HIRT
LINDA LU
LISA REIMER
LITA MICHAELS
LITTLE JIMMY
LIZ DAMON
LIZA GERMANO
LLOYD HARP
LONNIE LESTER
LONNIE MACK
LOREN "LO" WOODS
LOU COREY
LOUIE MC CANE
LOUIS COCHRAN
M. SHEETS
MA KELLY
MACHINE
MACUMBA DENTISTS
MADISON ZANE
MALACHI
MANCHILD
MANNY PARIS
MARC JOHNSON

MARCUS "LUCKY" HAMTON
MARDEN BAKER
MARK BENSON
MARK BERTRAM
MARK BINGHAM
MARK BOUSE
MARK BURTON
MARK BUSELLI
MARK CAWLEY
MARK CUTSINGER
MARK GALSTER
MARK HANCOCK
MARK KENNEDY
MARK MORAN
MARK PLUMMER
MARK STEINHARDT
MARK TRIBBY
MARK UTTER
MARLON JACKSON
MARTY BAKER
MARTY FORTSON
MARTY LAMBERT
MARTY MONAHAN
MARVIN CHANDLER
MARVIN SMITH
MARY MITCHELL
MARY MOSS
MAT CARTIN
MATHEMATICIANS
MATRIX
MATT DeVORE
MATT SPEAK
MATT THOMPSON
MATTHEW VAN- KERSEN
ME AND THEM GUYS
MEL JAMES (MELVIN
WALDEN)
MELTING POT
MELVIN EDMONDS
MELVIN RHYNE
MELVIN TURNER
MERT KING
MICHAEL BECK
MICHAEL BOARDS
MICHAEL BRANSON
MICHAEL BROWN
MICHAEL-CUNNINGHAM
MICHAEL GITLIN
MICHAEL JACKSON
MICHAEL KELSEY
MICHAEL MC FARLAND
MICHAEL REED
MICHAEL RYAN
MICHAEL STRICKLIN
MICKEY-KIRKPATRICK
MICKEY MACE
MICKEY SMITH
MIKE BERRY

MIKE BIDDLE
MIKE CALDWELL
MIKE CLARK
MIKE HALL
MIKE INGRAM
MIKE KISER
MIKE KOPACEK
MIKE LEKSE
MIKE MC GUYER
MIKE METZ
MIKE MILLIGAN
MIKE NICOLOFF
MIKE OST
MIKE RAY
MIKE RICHARDS
MIKE SHANE
MIKE SMITH
MIKE SULLIVAN
MIKE THOMAS
MIKE TUTTLE
MIKE UTTER
MIKE WANCHIC
MIKE'S HOUSE
MINGO JONES
MIXED COMPANY
MOBIUS STRIP
MONICA CANTRELL
MONIKA HERZIG
MONTE STOLTZ
MOONLIGHTERS
MORGAN-SCHUMACHER
MR SCIENCE
MR. "T"
MUDKIDS
MUSHROOM FARM
MYRIAD
MYRON MURRY
NANCY DORSEY
NAPTOWN PLAYERS
NATIONAL BISCUIT CO
ND WITNESS
NIAMBI STEELE
NICK SWEET RIVER JONES
NO LABELS
NO REGRETS
NOONEY (EVERETT) RICKETT
NORM LESTER
NORM SHAFET
NORM WHITNER
NORMANDIE
NOVA DELUXE
NOX
NYLE BROADEN
OLIVE LUCY
OLIVER MORRIS
OLIVER NELSON JR.
OPAL CORTNEY JR
ORLY KNUTSON

OTHER FIVE
OTIS JAYNE- MANSFIELD
OTTO NUSS
OVERLAND STAGE CO.
OVERLOAD
P. K. LAVENGOOD
P. S. DUMP YOUR
BOYFRIEND
P.J. & THE GENTRY
PAM LEE
PARADIGM
PASSION
PAT HAGENE
PAT MC ARDLE
PAT SMITH
PAT SNAY
PAT TRAVERS
PAT WO
PATRICK GLASS
PATTY RINDLES
PAUL BURTON
PAUL DENNERT
PAUL FRENTZ
PAUL GRAY
PAUL HMUROVICH
PAUL HOLDMAN
PAUL HUTCHINSON
PAUL JACKSON
PAUL PARKER
PAUL ROMINE
PAUL SCHAFER
PAUL SUROWIAK
PAUL TURNER
PAULA BARGE
PAULA OWEN
PEABODY
PEARLS
PEGGY MACK
PERRY CHOATE
PETE DUQUESNE
PETE SPECIAL
PETE WILHOIT
PETER KIENLE
PETER PILLS
PHAREZ WHITTED
PHIL ARMSTONG
PHIL BRAEDT
PHIL BRINES
PHIL FOSNAUGH
PHIL HUNDLEY
PHIL JACOBY
PHIL KELCH
PHIL MIDKIFF
PHIL PIERLE
PHIL RAMEY
PHIL T. BLUES
PHIL THOMPSON
PHILLIP SLAUGHTER

PHOENIX
PLAID DESCENT
PLAYMATE
PLEASANT STREET
POINT BLANK
PORT RASIN BAND
PRESIDENTS
PRIMEVIL
PROFILES
PULSAR
PURE FUNK
PURE GOLD
PUSH DOWN & TURN
R. WORTH
R.S.V.P.
RADIO FLYERS
RALPH COVERSTONE
RALPH MEYERS
RAMON
RANDY CREEP
RANDY DE FORD
RANDY HENDLEY
RANDY JOE DUKE
RANDY ZEHRINGER
RASPBERRY GRASSHOPPER
RASTABILLY REBELS
RAVENS
RAW MEAT
RAY CARRIER
RAY CHENOWITH
RAY CHOATE
RAY CHURCHMAN
RAY GADBERRY
RAY PETRONZIO
RAY SMITH
RAYFORD GRIFFIN
REB PORTER
RECORDIO
RED BEANS & RICE
RED GLANCE
REDCOATS
REGGIE GRIFFIN
REX CROCKETT
REX THOMAS
REX WAMSLEY
REX WILLIAMSON
RHONDA & THE TLC.
RHYTHM MACHINE
RICH GOOTEE
RICH KIDS
RICHARD "RICK"- FINCH
RICHARD OWENS
RICHIE BERMAN
RICHIE MARTIN
RICHIE MEDVESCEK
RICHIE NIVERSON
RICHIE SCHATZ
RICK & THE RIOTS

Let the Good Times Roll

RICK (DERRINGER) ZEHRINGER
RICK ALEXANDER
RICK BENICK
RICK CLAYTON
RICK FORTUNE
RICK INGLE
RICK LONG
RICK WEBSTER
RICK WILKERSON
RICK WORKMAN
ROADHOUSE
ROADMASTER
ROB DIXON
ROB LUCJAK
ROB MC COY
ROB SWEENY
ROBBIE MC VEY
ROBBIE WISE
ROBERT COLEMAN
ROBERT FETTIG
ROBERT PARSON
ROBERT PENICK
ROBERT RENOCK
ROBERT WESLEY
ROBERT YOUNG
ROBIN MC DOWELL
ROBIN REUTER
ROBIN STEELE
ROCK STRING BAND
ROCKY GIVANS
ROCKY HALL
ROD DERKS
ROD HANSEN
ROD KERSEY
ROD LITTLE
RODS N' CONES
RON "R.C." COFFMAN
RON BONHAM
RON BRINSON
RON CARROLL
RON CHANEY
RON COFFEY
RON COFFMAN
RON ENYARD
RON JACKSON
RON KNOOP
RON PERRY
RON RUSSELL
RON RUTJES
RON SCHROCK
RON SMITH
RONALD KHERT
RONDO LOSCHKY
RONNIE (HEGE) HAIG
RONNIE MATELIC
RONNIE SCHROCK
ROOKER & THE ROCKERS

ROOSEVELT JOHNSON
ROSS BARBOUR
ROXEN BOMBS
ROXIE PLETCHER
ROY ROBINETTE
ROYAL JONES & THE DUKES
ROYCE CAMPBELL
RUDY BARTLETT
RUDY ROSS
RUNNER WHITTEN
RUNNING ON EMPTY
RUSS JOHNSON
RUSS LEVITT
RUSS SANDERS
RUSSELL HAMPTON
RUSSELL TAYLOR
RUSSELL WEBSTER
RUSTY SAPP
RUSTY YORK
S. V. GRIDGESBY
SALLY'S DREAM
SALT & PEPPER
SAM GIBSON
SAM KING
SAMMY DEE
SANDER LEECH
SANDY GAY
SANGRALADS
SANZ INC
SARGE GLANTON
SCORE
SCOTT BAILEY
SCOTT BRANDT
SCOTT DAVIS
SCOTT GLEMSIECKE
SCOTT MC DOWELL
SCOTT MUSSELMAN
SCOTT SMITH
SCOTT WALLACE
SCOTT WOOLRIDGE
SCREAMIN' GYPSY BANDITS
SENTIMENTALS
SHADOW MYERS
SHADOWS OF SOUND
SHAPES
SHAWN PELTON
SHILOH MORNING
SHOOTING STARS
SHORTY SERGEANT
SHOTGUN
SID JENKINS
SILVER CREEK
SIM GRAVES
SINAMAX
SINDACATO
SIR WINSTON & THE COMMONS
SKEET BUSHOR

SKIP WAGNER
SKIP WALTERS
SLIDE HAMPTON
SMALL TALK
SMOKEY RAY
SNICKER
SONNY CHARLES
SONNY GRUBBS
SONNY JOHNSON
SONS OF SOUND
SOUDS UNLIMITED
SOUND REACTION
SPIDER HARRISON
SPIRTLES
SPRANGLED FRITILLA
SPURS RAGSDALE
STEELE
STEP WHARTON
STEPHEN MC NALLY
STEPHEN RILEY
STEVE "CROW"- HILKIN
STEVE ALLEE
STEVE BAKER
STEVE BALL
STEVE BENHAM
STEVE BROWN
STEVE BUTCHER
STEVE COTNER
STEVE DELONG
STEVE DOKKEN
STEVE DRYBREAD
STEVE FARBER
STEVE FEIKES
STEVE FIELDS
STEVE FISSEL
STEVE FOSSEN
STEVE FOSTER
STEVE HARDING
STEVE KINDER
STEVE KREIDER
STEVE LESTER
STEVE MICHAELS
STEVE NEPHEW
STEVE NEWBOLD
STEVE PRINCE
STEVE PRITCHARD
STEVE ROBBINS
STEVE ROBINETT
STEVE ROSS
STEVE SMITH
STEVE TAM
STEVE WALKER
STEVE WARINER
STEVE WEAKLEY
STEVE WOLF
STICKMAN
STONE SOUP
STRAITAWAYS

STUART DUNCAN	THE DAWNBEATS (2)	THE MARY JANES
STUTZ	THE DAWNELLS	THE MC COYS
STYLE	THE DEB TONES	THE MONOGRAMS
SUE HILL	THE DEPRESSIONS	THE MYSTERIES OF LIFE
SUNSET	THE DOMINOES	THE NEON NIGHTCRAWLERS
SUSIE PLETCHER	THE DOWNBEATS	THE NOBLEMEN
SWEETWATER	THE DUKES	THE ORIGINAL DUKES
SWINGIN' STING RAYS	THE DYNAMICS	THE OTHER FIVE
SY JONES	THE ENDD	THE OUTSIDERS
SYLVIA HUTTON	THE EPICS	THE PANICS
TAD ARMSTRONG	THE EQUALIZERS	THE PANTHERS
TAKERS	THE EYES	THE PASSION
TAY BOURQUEIN	THE FAITH BAND	THE PLAYBOYS
TEACH & THE TRACERS	THE FASCINATORS	THE PLETCHERS
TEACH THEROS	THE FERRIS WHEEL	THE POWER TRIO
TED BENNETH	THE FI-DELLS	THE PSYCHEDELIC ORANGES
TED HILL	THE FIFTH ADMENDMENT	THE RAMRODS
TED NIEMIEC	THE FIREFLIES	THE REFLECTIONS
TED PATTERSON	THE FIRST- IMPRESSION	THE RENEGADES
TED PITMAN	THE FIVE CHECKS	THE RHYTHM ROCKERS
TED TURNER	THE FIVE CORDS	THE RITUAL
TERRY COOK	THE FIVE STARS	THE RITZ BAND
TERRY HOWE	THE FOUR FRESHMEN	THE RIVIERAS
TERRY OGOLINI	THE FOUR SOUNDS	THE ROCKIN TONES
TERRY POTTS	THE FOUR WHEELS	THE ROYAL VIKINGS
TERRY TALBOT	THE GALAXIES	THE SAME
THE ACCENTS	THE GIZMOS	THE SANGRALADS
THE ALBINO FROGS	THE GOODTIMERS	THE SEVEN SEAS
THE ALL STAR FROGS	THE HAMILTON- MOVEMENT	THE SHADES
THE AMERICAN CAST		THE SHOWMEN
THE AQUANAUTS	THE HAMPTON- SISTERS	THE SHY ONES
THE ASCOTS	THE HAYMAKERS	THE SMOKE
THE BACKDOOR MEN	THE HEAVY	THE SPANIELS
THE BAD LANDS	THE HITCH-HIKERS	THE SPORTSMEN
THE BLUE ANGELS	THE IDLE FEW	THE STARLETTES
THE BLUE JEANS	THE ILLUSIONS	THE SUBURBANITES
THE BLUE TONES	THE IMPACTS	THE SUNSHINE WAY
THE BOPPERS	THE IMPOSTERS	THE SURF SUNS
THE BOSCO HEPCATS	THE INTRUDERS	THE SWAGMEN
THE BOYS NEXT DOOR	THE JACKSON FIVE	THE SWINGIN' LADS
THE CARDINALS	THE JACKSONS	THE TEEN TONES
THE CAVALIERS	THE JADES	THE THIRD DEGREE
THE CHAIN REACTION	THE JETSONS	THE TIKIS
THE CHECKMATES	THE JEWELS	THE TORKAYS
THE CHESSMEN	THE JIANTS	THE TRAVELLS
THE CHORDELLS	THE JUVENILES	THE TURBANS
THE CHOSEN FEW	THE KASTAWAYS	THE UNTOUCHABLES
THE CINDERS	THE KINSEY REPORT	THE VENDETTAS
THE CIRKIT	THE KNIGHTSMEN	THE VOLCANOES
THE CLASSMEN	THE KNOTS	THE VULGAR BOATMEN
THE CORKERS	THE LABELS	THE WAY
THE COUNTS	THE LAMBERTS	THE WHY STORE
THE COVEN	THE LAST FOUR- DIGITS	THE WILD THINGS
THE CRACKERJACKS	THE LAZY COWGIRLS	THE WIZZ KIDS
THE DAILY NEWS	THE LEMACS	THE WRIGHT- BROTHERS
THE DANCING CIGARETTES	THE LORDS OF LONDON	THE XL'S
THE DAWN FIVE	THE LOST SOULS	THELMA RUTH
THE DAWNBEATS	THE LYNX	THEM CHANGES

Let the Good Times Roll

THOM BRAUN
THOM WOODARD
THRUST
THURSTON HARRIS
TIGER WOOTEN
TIM AYERS
TIM BERRY
TIM BRICKLEY
TIM CARROLL
TIM FERGUSON
TIM NORTH
TIM WRIGHT
TIMEOUT
TIMMY BEAUMONT
TIMMY THOMAS
TIMOTHY NOE
TINA BARBIERI
TINA LANE
TINY VEE
TITO JACKSON
TOBIAS
TOBY MYERS
TOGETHERNESS IS
TOM BEALE
TOM BECKLEHIMER
TOM BEVEN
TOM CLARK
TOM DALEY
TOM HARDING
TOM KASCH
TOM KNAPP
TOM MOREHEAD
TOM MORIARITY
TOM MULLINEX
TOM REA
TOM RODGERS
TOM SIEVERS
TOM SPENCER
TOM WRIGHT
TOM YOUNG
TOMAS BADGER
TOMAS MITCHELL
TOMMY ADAMS
TOMMY BRANHAM
TOMMY FLINT
TOMMY LAM
TOMMY MULLINIX
TOMMY STILLWELL
TOMMY WILLS
TOMOKA ROAD
TON BENNETH
TONY BLACK
TONY GOODRICH
TONY HILDEBRAND
TONY LITTLE
TONY MEDEIROS
TONY NASSER
TORKAYS

TOXIC REASONS
TRANSPORTATION
TRINIA & THE GYPSIES
TRINIA COX
TRIPLE PLAY
TRISH AKERS
TROY SEELE
TROY SHONDELL
T-TEXAS TYLER
TURNER BROTHERS
TUTTLE & THE SHELLS
VANGUARDS
VEGAS
VICKIE DANIELS
VICKY RICHMOND
VINCE SANDERS
VINCENT STEWART
VIRGIL JONES
VIRTUE HAMPTON
VISCAYNES
VOICES
VOYAGER
VULGAR BOATMEN
W. RAY JOHNSON
WALLY MURPHY
WALT REED
WALTER "ARKIE"- BITTLE
WALTER STONE
WANDA
WANDA MICHELI
WAYNE FISHER
WAYNE HALL
WAYNE WILSON
WE – 3
WENDY REED
WES BEAM
WES MONTGOMERY
WHY ON EARTH
WILD ONES
WILD THINGS
WILLIAM BAILEY (AXL
ROSE)
WILLIAM BOYD
WILLIAM VAN BUSKIRK
WILLIE (PHILLIPS)- JONES
WILLIE BAKER
WILLIS C. JACKSON
WINTON REYNOLDS
WONDERDRUG
WORDS OF WISDOM
XAX
YELLOW DOG
YOUNG SET
YUN HUI
ZANNA MITCHELL
ZERFAS
ZERO BOYS

Let the Good Times Roll

Let the Good Times Roll